Starve The Ego: Feed The Soul!

Souldrama®: Ignite Your Spiritual Intelligence!

Starve The Ego: Feed The Soul!

Souldrama®: Ignite Your Spiritual Intelligence!

Author

Connie Miller

www.souldrama.com

ISBN: 978-0-557-25972-4

For Our Children and Grandchildren

Disclaimer

The author makes no warranties expressed or implied that these techniques will produce positive results for every individual. These skills are meant to be used under the supervision of a professional trained in the use of the techniques of psychodrama and group psychotherapy. In offering the techniques of training for Souldrama® the author is not providing any individualized advice to any person. The author disclaims any liability or loss with the techniques and advice therein. Any names used in the contents of the story are purely coincidental.

BY: Connie Miller, MS, CP, NCC, LPC
International Institute of Souldrama®
620 Shore Rd
Spring Lake Heights, New Jersey 07762 USA
www.souldrama.com
e mail: connie@souldrama.com
732-974-1978

Do not feed your ego and your problems, with your attention. ...Slowly, surely, the ego will lose weight, until one fine day it will be nothing but a thin ghost of its former self. You will be able to see right through it, to the divine presence that shines in each of us." Eknath Easwaran.

Contents

Foreword

Please Do Not Feed the Ego!

"Souldrama®" came into being as a result of a powerful workshop, "Healing with the Energy of Angels" that I conducted in Sedona, Arizona, in April, 1997 with Stevan Thayer. Stevan contributed his work of Integrated Energy ® called "Healing with the Energy of Angels"® and I contributed the concepts of group therapy, sociometry, and psychodrama. This method provided the spark of creativity for a new healing technique called Souldrama®, an action technique which (Miller, 2000) integrated spirituality and psychology. Souldrama is similar to the stages of a pilgrimage or rite of passage that integrates all three levels of intelligences, our rational, emotional, and spiritual, aligning the ego and soul to create spiritually intelligent leadership to help us access a "UQ" or universal intelligence.

Stevan Thayer, incorporated into the workshop a mental concept of a framework of six multiple stages of spiritual growth and healing, which he delineated by "veils". Each veil had a purpose and the end result was to align the ego and soul so one could discover his or her higher purpose. By developing and expanding Stevan's mental concept of the veils, I combined the clinical methods of psychodrama to move my clients from co-dependency to co-creativity. I changed the concept of the veils to fit seven sequential doorways or passageways to spiritual transformation with each doorway having a purpose, challenge, and a gift while leading us through a transitional space to transpersonal consciousness (Miller 2000). As the concept of Souldrama® began to spread worldwide, I began to use the concept of the archetypes of Light Messengers© along with the seven doorways. Thanks go to Bobbi Torres for creating these Light Messengers,© prayers, and symbols for the sole purpose of Souldrama. I believe in using the mind, body, and spirit to heal; thus, Souldrama incorporates all three of these modalities which correspond to our rational, emotional, and spiritual intelligences.

Putting Spirituality into Action

My original idea was to create an action method for spirituality that could be brought into a physical format of a structured group action mode of healing in the field of psychology. Souldrama is an outgrowth of working for years with codependency. I designed this method for clients who were "stuck" in life. Many of my clients had either a successful career or relationship; they were unaware that they could have both. The primary purpose of this method moves clients past resistance and helps them to erase the blocks that prevent them from reaching and living their higher purpose. It is also designed to help transform the wounds that they suffered from their childhoods into spiritual gifts (Miller, 2000), while allowing them to discover and change their internal image of a higher power to one that is more loving. Souldrama® integrates spirituality into the psychodramatic process with the structure of the doors and moves psychodrama to another level, that of the transpersonal.

The Therapeutic Factor

As a therapist, there were times that I felt "stuck" within myself. I found this to be a common problem in my profession. I was left searching for "creative" solutions to clinical problems. Traditionally, brief time- limited approaches to therapy are aimed at treating specific symptoms, rather than dealing with issues of a deeper, more personal, more spiritual nature. When clients came to see me, they were often feeling personally diminished, disconnected from others, spiritually impoverished, as well as anxious and depressed. Addressing these deeper more spiritual issues effected lasting change. Many treatment programs minimize or discourage the importance of spirituality, especially when the treatment in question is aimed primarily at symptom relief.

Spirituality can be viewed as an energy that frames our experience of being in the world. When we access that energy, it empowers us with courage to resolve problems and provides faith to move forward in life. Through putting spirituality into action, we can access this creative energy to help others make meaningful life changes. One of the most effective ways to tap into that creativity is to broaden the client's frame of reference from the literal to the metaphorical. People's inner logic seems to be best expressed through metaphors, symbols, fantasies, rituals, and stories. These are powerful channels for changing people's perceptions and experiences. These spiritually action-based interventions are geared toward helping others as they overcome blocks to experiencing a happy, fulfilled life. Through the use of methods such as myth, metaphor, guided meditation, energy work, and prayer, people may begin to realign their ego and soul to access disassociated spiritual energy (Miller, 2007). Through the spark of spirituality, it is my hope that we can all overcome problems ranging from relationship, career, and prosperity problems to reach our higher purpose and become spiritually intelligent leaders.

Moreno (1889-1974) was the father of psychodrama. He believed that as human beings, we are fundamentally beings of action, and we have hungers for action that, until satisfied clinically, will seek to gratify themselves in life. He sought to create a clinical environment through which these "act hungers" could be explored and resolved on the clinical stage with understanding and insight reflected back. Like Aristotle, he felt that if pain could be "purged" dramatically, it would reduce the inclination to recreate dysfunctional relationship dynamics in life (Moreno, 1946). Witnessing the power of the group to heal and the powerful results of a healing modality in which thinking, feeling, and behavior could be explored and reintegrated in a clinical forum, Moreno created his methods of psychodrama, sociometry, and group psychotherapy (Moreno, 1946, 1972). Psychodrama makes the expansion of reality possible by methods not used in life. Moreno believed that there is no healing other than that which comes from the group itself. He believed that an individual has no authority in a group. The power of a group, he felt, came from the religion of its anonymity and of just being embraced by love in the moment. He believed that we all have the collective responsibility of continuing the works of our creator to become all we can be and not be limited by the cultural conserves of society (Moreno, 1946). As a trainer, educator, and practitioner of psychodrama, I have thoroughly incorporated his ideas into my work with Souldrama.

Since I think more in terms of my right brain, it is easier for me to present my ideas in this book to you in the form of a story. While doing so, my own spontaneity and creativity are continually being accessed, as well as all of my intelligences. It seems that the deeper I am awakened, the more I feel incompetent. And this in turn creates more need to surrender to divine grace and help. My biggest lesson in life has been that I cannot heal alone. My own ego has been on a diet many times and at times has been very fat. Hopefully, as you read this book and experience this process, your ego will get thinner to see the divine within. I hope you enjoy the story.

Introduction

A human being is a part of the whole, called by us 'Universe,' a part limited in time and space. He experiences himself, his thoughts and feelings as something separated from the rest - a kind of optical delusion of his consciousness. This delusion is a kind of prison for us, restricting us to our personal desires and to affection for a few persons nearest to us. Our task must be to free ourselves from this prison by widening our circle of compassion to embrace all living creatures and the whole of nature in its beauty. Nobody is able to achieve this completely, but the striving for such achievement is in itself a part of the liberation and a foundation for inner security." -Albert Einstein-

There is No "I" in IQ

Today, we seem to search for meaning and purpose in our lives and begin a spiritual journey as we ask ourselves…is this all there is? In troubled times, new approaches and new initiatives are needed to break through the present impasse to restore health and vibrancy. Awakening consciousness is the foundation for the change we seek to see in the world. Peace building strategies are essential in a world that is encumbered with conflict, tension, injustice, and constantly changing circumstances. People are living longer today, and later in our lives, there is much interest in spirituality as we try to reconnect within and to each other. Whether we call it following our spiritual journey, or living a more meaningful and loving life, it is all about responding to the basic impulse that draws us to become more conscious and compassionate within ourselves and toward others.

We live in a materialistic and literal culture that lacks vision and imagination and most importantly, soul. Our world needs more soul, more meaning. We, as conscious beings, have, as our primary responsibility, the task of bringing soul into the world. We must first do this within ourselves, our own personal worlds, and in all our relationships. Then we must bring soul into the world through our work and higher purpose. In short, we must become good spiritual leaders.

We are all agents of change. The task of this generation is to cut through the illusion that we live in separate worlds. If we want to change systems, we have to change human behavior; however, human behavior is not so easily changed. The main responsibility of a spiritual leader today is to change the motivations that drive behavior, enabling people to achieve real transformation. Long- term mental and emotional health requires more than a temporary reduction of symptoms. What seems to be required is a higher consciousness, or a spiritual intelligence, from which a larger sense of self can be derived. One way to do this is to move from our rational intelligence to our spiritual intelligence. This involves changing the "I" in the IQ to a more universal intelligence or "UQ". Then we will be able to awaken our higher purpose and create spiritually intelligent leadership that embraces all of our intelligences to awaken our higher purpose that unites rather than separates us from others.

If we want to become spiritual leaders, is important to continue our own spiritual journey. Many of us need a safe place to go to learn a new way along with new creative tools to find a way to help us to access our spiritual intelligence and create spiritually intelligent leadership. We all want to make a difference, to know our life has been worthwhile. However, we cannot make a lasting difference at home and in the world unless we do so from a higher level of consciousness than our personalities. This higher level is soul life, our essence.

Turning on higher intelligence is not only fun and joyous, it is absolutely necessary if we and our intelligent civilization are to survive the coming decades. By higher intelligence, I mean the whole universal intelligence, not just greater intellect, but greater emotional sanity, love, compassion, creativity, inspiration, and especially the inspirational experiences.

All previous cultures have held basically the same ideas about spirit: There is an infinite invisible world beyond the world we know and experience, and our mission in life is to discover this infinite world and our purpose in life. Some, like I, call this infinite world a Greater Wholeness of Being, or God. To experience divinity is actually a simple thing as divinity is ever present. The problem is our consciousness; we need to simplify our consciousness to experience the divine in all things, to return home and back to our spiritual intelligence.

The ego developed in early childhood can obstruct or distort one's relationship with the divine. It can manifest a far richer consciousness in everyday life if brought into alignment with the soul.

The Purpose of Souldrama®

In attempting to heal the human personality, we have witnessed a rift between psychology and spirituality for generations. The two have been at opposite polarities and it is becoming evident that this separation is farther from the truth. Lasting healing can occur when an individual's psychological and spiritual health can be seen as one. For this we must take a spiritual journey aligning our ego and soul. Our ego is our personality that experiences separation and limitation where we live in a material world of form, distortion, illusion, and pain. Our soul embraces unity and wholeness and can work with cause instead of effects. Anytime we separate ourselves from others, we know our personality or ego is in control. Our ego focuses on how we are different from the world, and our soul focuses on how we are the same. When we align these two aspects of ourselves, we can move forward to our higher purpose, to our soul's mission. When we have a strong and healthy personality, we can become capable of expressing our soul and work in alignment toward our higher purpose. We can begin to touch our hearts and not our minds.

Many methods rationally tell us that we need to align these two aspects of ourselves but few provide a psychotherapeutic action model to demonstrate how to align the two. Souldrama® provides us with such a model. What is needed is an action process to unravel our IQ structure as not being one that is only rational, but three- dimensional, including Emotional IQ and Spiritual IQ. We need our Rational IQ, but ignoring the heart and only paying attention to the mind can cause suffering, worry, and anxiety. If we only function by the heart, we will not be able to control our impulses. We need a balance between the head and the heart as well as all three intelligences so that we can see the sacred in everyday life and in all we do, from our careers to our relationships in all of society.

Wholeness involves bringing together what has been separated. This is the meaning of integration. A soul under stress sacrifices parts of itself. True healing involves helping a person to gradually re-own and re-integrate any of the severed aspects of self- love, courage, a sense of empowerment, sexuality, spiritual connectedness, humility, surrender, tenderness, and independent thinking. Helping people redefine themselves by putting the focus inward toward their divine selves and back toward their spontaneity and creativity in turn enables them to develop a relationship with their higher selves. We all want to be seen, be heard, and to belong. Obviously, if we want connection, we need people. As such, Souldrama is a group process. If we begin to read the books alone and do the work alone on the Internet, we are separating ourselves from others. This is what keeps feeding the ego.

Souldrama may be compared to a pilgrimage allowing one to process any change in life with conscious awareness of what we leave behind, and it also provides a guide to facilitate entering the unknown of what lies ahead. Souldrama® helps one to (1) accept the call to journey for a specific purpose; (2) find the faith in one's vision needed to set out; (3) learn how to invoke the strength of spirit; (4) allow the spirit to speak and work through you in order to persevere; (5) overcome the obstacles whose intentions are to slow you down or to stop you; (6) perform the appropriate rituals, enact the mythology, and connect with the transcendent self, upon arrival at the destination of the pilgrimage, and (7) return to one's home community as a spiritual leader, bringing back the blessings and enlightenment obtained. Souldrama puts spirituality into action and gives structure to the process of recovery while integrating the right and left brain through action methods. It is especially helpful to remove the blocks in our careers and relationships.

This book offers an action method that aligns our spiritual and rational intelligences or our egos and souls so that we can become co-creators with our Higher Power, awaken our higher purpose, and remove the blocks that are keeping us stuck in relationships and our careers. When these blocks are removed, we can become spiritually intelligent leaders. It is not a substitute for therapy but merely a model to serve to integrate all three intelligences so that we can form a universal intelligence by putting spirituality into action (Miller, 2008). If you are ready to risk the transformation, this book will provide you with an outline for Souldrama. It is meant to only be an outline, as the real work comes through taking the risk in an action workshop with others. When we take the risk to change, we can remember that true spiritual growth means letting go of our opinions and false beliefs, developing faith, surrendering and totally shifting our identity, and changing our perceptions that ultimately we believed constituted our identity. As your ego becomes thinner, you will feel like you are dying, when in fact you are only transforming and will feel more alive than ever. You will become a child again, a playful being in the universe, and not self-consciousness. You will remember that the universe is friendly and blessing us constantly.

Many of us try to hear God through the mind when we really need to hear God through the heart. God cannot be understood, comprehended, or experienced through the mind. The mind identifies with who we "think" we are, while the path of the heart requires letting go of the mind, letting go of the ego, letting go of the "I," while in turn letting go of control. This allows us to see with our awakened purpose what a truly loving God would like us to be.

A Story

This is a story about relationships. A story about a man named Iye I.Q. who lives in the land of Rational Intelligence, in the state of Ego. Iye desires to take a spiritual pilgrimage to meet the girl of his dreams Skye, S.Q., who lives in the land of Spiritual Intelligence, in the state of Soul. In our story, we will help Iye take a pilgrimage to reach Skye by journeying into and through the seven doors of spiritual transformation of Souldrama, so that his ego can reconnect with his soul and his rational intelligence can reconnect with his spiritual intelligence. Each time Iye passes through a doorway of transformation, he will have a challenge to complete, and at the completion, he will receive a gift to take with him into the next door of transformation. Only after he has discovered his true self and has aligned his own ego and soul, integrated all three levels of intelligences; the rational, emotional, and spiritual, will he will meet Skye, live in the present with purpose and be open to truly see the girl of his dreams. Then they can move together into the new land of UQ, or universal intelligence. Through this process, Iye will need to let go of his ego and surrender so he can learn that when the ego and soul are aligned, there is no "I" in IQ but a universal UQ, or universal intelligence. Will he complete the journey?

My idea of taking a good spiritual path and becoming a good spiritual leader is helping and supporting people to trust in themselves and their personal connections with a higher power. When we can find these connections, there are no more rules, as life is ever-changing and spontaneously evolving. We are always challenged to develop new aspects of ourselves and since everyone's spiritual path is different, we need to give each other hope and encouragement. Ask yourself now, where am I on my path? If you are ready, we will begin our journey with Iye.

Chapter One

Meeting Iye in the State of Ego

"Why can't I ever find a relationship that lasts? Why do I fell so alone and that something is missing in my life? Why can't I find the girl of my dreams?" This was Iye's familiar lament.

Iye's last breakup with the woman in his life was so painful that he invited me into the land of Rational Intelligence to present a Souldrama® workshop. At first, I resisted revisiting the state of Ego for I remember how unhappy I had been there. I am a bit wiser now for I know that every time I resist something, I am given an opportunity to grow. So here I was back in the land of Rational Intelligence, in the state of Ego, wondering again what I was doing here.

Iye met me at the airport and the first thing I noticed when I arrived was that although the land looked very fertile, there were no flowers or gardens. When I pointed this out, Iye said *"Everyone is busy preparing the soil, turning it over and over and creating fences and boundaries for their gardens and perfecting the seeds. They are always planning for every possible problem that could happen when the garden is planted; therefore, the seeds never get planted! They stay on the shelf."*

"This seems to be a metaphor for life" I told Iye. "If we never take the action to plant the seeds, our gardens will never grow. The seeds are our creativity - our life's purpose - the part of our soul that needs nourishing and growth. In our recovery process, the missing piece is the planting of the seeds. This is the part of life that offers forward movement with the energy of joy."

Even though Iye, age 50, had been in recovery from Alcoholism for the past 15 years, he could not seem to get his relationships right. Iye had a successful career as a prominent research scientist for the past 25 years. Having been divorced twice he, was bored with life, felt isolated and often depressed in his job, and unhappy in his relationships. He has two children from his second marriage a boy Chet age 13 and a girl, Sage, age 11. His hobby is photography. All Iye can think about is his next relationship and how when he meets the girl of his dreams, everything will be fine.

Iye cannot meet the girl of his dreams because for him, dreaming is more fun than the reality of a relationship. You see, when he dreams, he can control the beginning and endings. When he actually gets into a relationship, he has to deal with the reality. There he has no control.

Iye suffers from what I have coined "IDD" Internal Dialogue Disorder. He is very busy figuring out every possible problem that could occur from any action he may take and the problems from any future actions. As a result, Iye does not live in the present and is too afraid to move forward in a life that now has no meaning or purpose. He is afraid to plant his own garden. Further, he often asks, "Is this all there is?"

Iye's father was an engineer. He was a very quiet man until he was provoked by Iye's mother, a very emotional woman. When his mother, a teacher of romance languages could not get an emotional response from his father, she would provoke him until he exploded. Some response, she thought, was better than nothing. His father then would just start to drink and isolate. Isolation became a pattern of how to deal with emotions within this family.

As an only child, Iye would go to his room and isolate when his parents fought. He would sit on his bed and look out the window and just think. He would go up into his head and try to figure out what was happening. When the lights went out he would worry and become hyper vigilant. To stop himself from feeling and worrying, he would distract himself reading for hours finding safety in his books and in words. His books and his mind were his constant companion. They were his friends. Later, he turned to photography to capture moments of beauty and love.

In order to get his father's full attention, Iye would do research in one of his books and present him with any new fact or information. His father then would notice him and give him some attention. What he learned was that in order to get love from his father, he had to have a lot of new facts and information. He therefore took on the role of "information getter" for his father.

Iye did not look for his mother's attention, rather tried to avoid her and when he had to be in her presence, he learned to mostly tolerate her. She was always smothering him, trying to find an emotional companion and confidant. She would pour out her feelings about his father's behavior and his lack of emotion. Iye learned to avoid his mother as much as possible because he did not want to be smothered nor hear about his father's inadequacies. Thus, he learned how to leave situations that required intimacy for fear of engulfment. He developed two main roles in life in order to survive in this family; the avoider or distancer and the information gatherer.

"You have a very interesting name, Iye, does it have a meaning?"

"Yes, he said. In Native American language it means "Smoke".

"Well, let's hope that this process can help you begin to see clearly!"

Our Rational Intelligence and our Brains

We sat down to have lunch and Iye asked *"Why can't I move forward in a relationship? I seem to find the same woman with the same problems? Why can't I find true love and the relationship of my dreams? Why can't I commit or find anyone? I feel so alone."*

Because I was in the land of logic and words, it was important to answer in a way that Iye could understand to satisfy his ego and his rational mind. I knew, living in this state that he would need to be offered a lot of concrete proof. "First Iye, let's talk about our brains and how we think. Then we will talk about our intelligences, especially our Rational Intelligence." Iye was not aware that his thinking was controlled primarily by left brain.

World famous neurologist, Sperry (1969), won a Nobel Prize for his groundbreaking research on human brain functions. Sperry was totally surprised to find that people had a tendency to use one hemisphere of the brain more than the other. When Sperry began his research in the early 1950s, he concluded that individuals were either predominantly left-brain users or right-brain users. Sperry had set out to determine which particular part or parts of the brain were involved in specific mental tasks. We know now that the left brain hemisphere is predominantly involved in the mathematical, logical, analytic, and academic tasks. These tasks may involve linear thinking and making use of alphabets, numbers, scales, lists, etc. The left brain deals with inputs, one at a time, processes information in a linear and sequential manner, deals with time, is responsible for verbal expression and language, and for invariable and arithmetic operations. It specializes in recognizing words and numbers and does logical and analytical thinking and is the seat of reason."

'This sounds just like me!'

"To go on, the left brain is interested in details, analyses, and a detached intellectual perspective of events and experiences. This part of our brain controls our rational intelligence." We stopped and rested on a bench and I took out a picture of the brain. "Look at this picture."

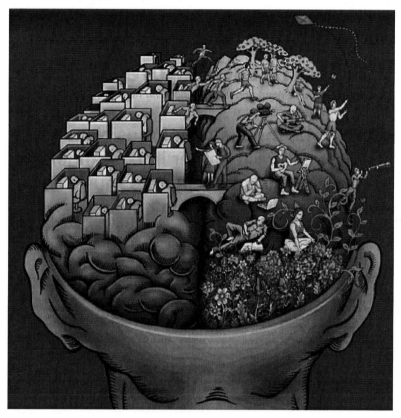

www.brainbasedbusiness.com illustration

"Everything that appears in the universe had its origin in mind. Mind evolves ideas, and ideas express themselves through thoughts and words. We call this our rational intelligence, RQ, and it is often measured by IQ tests (Intelligence Quotient). The word intelligence means to learn and understand deal with new situations. (Langenscheidt, 1999)

Rational Intelligence is a person's capacity to acquire knowledge (i.e. learn and understand), apply knowledge (solve problems), and engage in abstract reasoning. It is the power of one's intellect, and as such is clearly a very important aspect of one's overall well-being. Psychologists have attempted to measure it for well over a century."

"What is the IQ that is often measured?" asked Iye.

"Intelligence Quotient (IQ) is the score you get on an intelligence test. Originally, it was a quotient (a ratio): IQ= MA/CA x 100 [MA is mental age, CA is chronological age]. Today, scores are calibrated against norms of actual population scores."

"This I can understand. Now you are talking my language."

"Here in the land of Rational Intelligence, in the state of Ego, is where you reside now and your thinking is controlled by your left brain."

"Yes and I feel like I am always missing something. But I am excellent in my job and I get many awards for scientific research."

"You have many talents that work well for you in your career, but how well do these talents work in relationships?"

"Not very well, I guess that is why I asked you to come here. Women always say that I am boring and not at all spontaneous."

"Tell me about the woman of your dreams"

"She will be able to express her emotions, be sensuous, passionate, and philosophical and be able to get the whole picture of our experiences. She won't worry about things all the time and be playful and spontaneous. She will have lots of energy and live in the present."

"It sounds like you are looking for woman who uses predominately their right brain. The right brain hemisphere, as you can see, is involved predominantly in creative and artistic tasks which involve images, colors, shapes, sounds, rhythm, etc. The right brain is interested in the whole rather than the details or the parts. Here there is no separation and everything is one. The right brain appreciates the sensuous, philosophical, and emotional aspects of our experiences. This is the part of the brain that controls our spiritual intelligence or SQ. This can be found in the land of Soul where the girl of your dreams resides. The woman you are looking for lives in a land that is lush and green. She is continually planting seeds and allows them to be randomly be sown by the wind. They grow where they may and by not trying to control the outcome she understands that each seed has a purpose."

"In other words a rose will always be a rose. Please tell me more about her!"

"The right brain can integrate many inputs at once, processes information more diffusely and simultaneously, deal with space, be responsible for gestures, facial movements, and body language, relational operations, recognizes places, faces, objects, and music. Because she thinks with her right brain, she can do intuitive and holistic thinking. This side of the brain is the seat of passion and dreams. In fact, the girl of your dreams is probably an artist, craftswoman, or musician."

"She sounds so different than me! So she is not just a dream?"

"No you just forgot she was there. There is a saying I use in relationships, "If two of you are the same then one of you is unnecessary!" This means that it is fine to be different as this is a way for us to grow and learn and to help each other heal."

"How do I get to her? Show me the books and I will figure it out."

"In order to get to the land of Soul, you must bridge the gap. This means you must begin a spiritual journey to the land of Soul. In between the left and right brain, is a gap. This is where the emotional intelligence lies, or the EQ. It must be bridged to reach the land of Soul. This is not something you can do alone. If you try to do this journey alone, you will not meet the girl of your dreams for it is in relationships that we see ourselves. I will talk more about our Emotional Intelligence later. Let me assure you that we will continue to discuss our intelligences and I will continue to give you facts and proof as we move along on our pilgrimage. We need to integrate and balance all three of our intelligences to become a spiritually intelligent leader and this involves aligning the ego and the soul."

"How do I do this?"

"Our first step is to stop feeding the ego with thoughts, judgments, and comparisons and put it on a diet."

Our Intelligences

"Was I always this way?"

"No. Not as a child. Let me give you an example of when you used to use all your intelligences. Your brain is just like your car. If the wheels on the left side of your car are in top condition, but the right side wheels are jammed, your car can't go very far. You need both sides of the wheels turning together for an efficient ride. Likewise, let the wheels of your mind, the right side as well as the left side, turn together so they can support each other. You did use all of your intelligences when you were very young. When you were a child, you explored an object, using all of your senses. You touched touch the object at hand, felt it, saw it from every angle, and shook it to see if it made any sound. You were excited by the colors, shapes, and movement and tried to manipulate the objects in several different ways. The fact was you were not merely using the left or the right brain, but the whole brain.

For example, as adults, we marvel at how good children are with computers and phone technology. Part of the reason is that their whole brain is involved in "playing" with computers. As a result of this, children learn and remember more than adults do. For example, we can talk and read about the proper techniques of how to surf, (not the web) but until we actually get in the water and take the action will we get wet, feel the water and movement of the waves, and actually surf. The rational IQ is teaching us how to surf, the emotional IQ deals with the feeling of being in the water including all your present and past fears related to your first memories of swimming, and SQ with the motion and being at one during the movement when mind, body, and spirit are all working together and we are totally in the present."

"I have always been afraid of the water ever since I saw a friend of mine almost drown, but I play video games and use the internet for hours! I am really good at that! I can become one with the video games."

"What I just noticed is that as soon as you talked about your friend, you began to talk about video games. We will talk more about the feelings you had when you saw your friend almost drown later when we enter emotional intelligence. Feelings are a problem in the land of ego. The video games are something that gives you pleasure and that pleasure or distraction comes from outside of yourself. Gary Small, (2008), author of *I Brain: Surviving the Technological Alteration of the Modern Mind*, said that digital immersion can cause loss of social connections that protect us from stress and videos games, while they improve eye hand coordination, may also suppress the frontal lobe of the brain hindering memory, problem solving skills, and attention. The challenge in anything is to find the right balance. But let's get back to memory before I get distracted.

Memory works better when you use the whole brain. Take for example the task of memorizing a list of items. Try making a list of the items on this table. Look at it and memorize it. In two days, you may forget it. You were using the left brain. Now let me change the objects on the table. Make another list but memorize the list in a different way, deciding to involve your right brain as well by using vision, imagination, and by being creative. Make pictures in your mind's eye as you memorize the items. Generously use colors, humor, and action in the scene you draw in your mind. All these are right brain memory. After two days see for yourself which one is easier to retain in your memory. If you memorize the list by involving your whole brain, you will remember the items in the exact order for a long time. To memorize in this fashion is to use the whole brain."

"So how will the Souldrama workshop help me?"

"If we want to integrate all our intelligences, we must use a method that uses all parts of the brain. Souldrama uses action methods involving the mind body and spirit to access all parts of the brain to help you heal. When we do the work in a Souldrama workshop, we are using all parts of the brain and taking action so that our healing work also becomes our play. Thus, it is remembered."

"But I am very smart and I have done amazing research for science, in fact I have a very high intelligence quotient."

"Yes", I agreed, "maybe now it is the time to talk more about our ego in relationship to our intelligences. Every time we try to measure ourselves, we are labeling ourselves as "I am smart", etc. It is then we begin to compare ourselves against others and the judgment process begins. This feeds the ego. The truth is that we have many types of intelligences and there are many ways to develop those intelligences."

"Good, I need more proof," said Iye.

"What else" I thought to myself. Now I was being judgmental. "Let me offer some ideas about our intelligence's, Iye.

"Gardner (1999) recognized that humans have not just one but multiple intelligences and he speculated about the following ten possibilities as discreet intelligences:

- Linguistic/verbal intelligence, involves sensitivity to spoken and written language and the ability to learn languages;
- Logical/mathematical intelligence, involves the capacity to analyze problems logically, solve math problems, and investigate issues scientifically;
- Musical intelligence, which refers to skill in the performance, composition, and appreciation of musical patterns;
- Body-kinesthetic intelligence, using the whole or parts of the body to solve problems or fashion products;

- Spatial intelligence, which is the ability to recognize and manipulate patterns in space;
- Interpersonal intelligence, which is the capacity to understand the intentions, motivations, and desires of other people and work effectively with them;
- Intrapersonal intelligence, which is the capacity to understand oneself and to use this information effectively in regulating one's life;
- Naturalist intelligence, which is expertise in the recognition and classification of the flora and fauna of one's environment;"

"So I this is what I use when I do my photography?"

"Yes. Along with:

- Spiritual intelligence, the ability to master a set of diffuse and abstract concepts about being, and also mastering the craft of altering one's consciousness in attaining a certain state of being. It is an "intelligence that explores the nature of existence in its multifarious guises" (Gardner, 1999, p. 60); and

- Existential intelligence, "the capacity to locate oneself with respect to the furthest reaches of the cosmos the infinite and infinitesimal--and the related capacity to locate oneself with respect to such existential features of the human condition as the significance of life, the meaning of death, the ultimate fate of the physical and the psychological worlds and such profound experiences as love of another person or total immersion in a work of art" (Gardner, 1999, p. 61). There are in addition many other ideas of our intelligences."

"Wow," said Iye, "so if I do not integrate my own intelligences, love, on a profound level is not possible! So how can I get to the land of Spiritual Intelligence?

"Iye, this is not something you have to" get to "but something you forgot that you already have. You have only created blocks in your own mind that stop you from accessing it. This is how come you called me here. "

"When I am in nature, taking photographs of scenery, or of animals, I have no idea of time. So when do this it is like being in a trance, I forget about time."

"When you do this, it is involving all parts of your brain. The trance has been what you have been in since childhood when you forgot who you were, I am trying to wake you up, not get you to dream."

"Can you tell me more about this spiritual journey I am about to take to integrate all three of my intelligences?"

"Let me give you a quote from Stephen Covey (1989): "Everything -- absolutely everything -- that happens in our lives has a spiritual cause. Events on all other levels -- mental, emotional and physical -- are only effects. When we are struggling with any challenge, whether it is ill health, a lack of money, a lost job, relationships, an accident, whatever -- we need to look for the spiritual learning. We can ask ourselves, "What quality does my soul want me to live more fully? If you start to think the problem is 'out there,' stop yourself. That thought is the problem ".

"Keep this in mind as we move on. How about having some lunch? I am getting hungry in fact I notice my hunger seems to be even greater in this land of Ego."

> *To be taught is nothing; everything is inside waiting to be awakened.*
>
> *-Paracelsus -*

Chapter Two

My Big Fat Ego

We journeyed on to have lunch. I knew Iye would want to ask many questions knowing the land we were in. I also noticed that he was carrying many books.

Iye: *"Tell me more about the ego what is that? I know I live in this state but I know so little about it."*

"Some people say that the ego means *Edging God Out* or some people have referred to it as *Earth Guide Only*. The ego, or your personality, speaks in terms of words or rational intelligence (what I think). Words reduce reality to something the human mind can grasp. Words can never describe in depth the ultimate purpose of your life or your experiences or even who you are. Words cannot describe the feeling you have when you look at your children or the moment you see a beautiful sunset in nature. The ego is who you think you are, the false "I" or the illusory sense of self or as Einstein said "an optical illusion of consciousness." When we move through our rational intelligence, we can dis-identify from our thoughts and there is a feeling of the thoughts shifting from being the content in your mind to being in the background. In the land of Ego, we are very busy trying to define and communicate who think we are and the soul is busy trying to communicate to the ego that we truly are. The ego gets so fat; it cannot see its divine self."

"In other words I am not really who I think I am? And this woman is trying to reach me but my head gets in the way?"

"Yes."

"As the workshop get closer, I am more fearful. What is this about?"

"This is about letting go of our egos and changing the illusion of who we think we are. Sometimes it is hard to change, and we often resist when the opportunity comes along. We have many ways to avoid change; indecision, ambivalence, and procrastination - for with change comes unpredictability, disorder, confusion, and chaos. Sometimes we jump headfirst impulsively into new situations and relationships to distract ourselves from changing and feeling." Iye emphatically nodded his head in agreement! "In the land of Ego, we like to be in control of the outcome of our relationships. Another reason we do not want to change is because we will have to grieve the losses that will result from moving forward. This is when we need to ask ourselves: "Who will be most affected by my changing"? For instance, one client of mine refuses to leave his girlfriend who has no spiritual path and is haunted by "If I move on, I will have to leave her behind. How will she ever make it without me? I am irreplaceable!" People can hold themselves back because they don't want to release the very obstacle keeping them from moving forward. This is an irrational need for security, for control, or for the status of the social role that comes with the relationship.

Compare change to a football game. Imagine that each time when you play football you get beat up, bruised and battered. and you hardly ever win. After the game, your body feels terrible. But you know how to play the game and continue to do so because you know all the rules and in which direction to run. You also know how you will feel when the game is finished. The outcome is predictable. Suppose you began to bounce the ball when you receive it and begin to play basketball! All of a sudden, you decide that this is more fun and you are not getting hurt. Would you try and create a game of basketball or would you go back to the old game because you knew how to play and how you would feel after the game? "

"I don't know if I could win playing basketball".

"Exactly. We like to predict the outcome so that we can stay in our old roles and stay in control. We need to ask ourselves "are we really winning?" Or could it be possible that just like in our spiritual development, the more players we find to play basketball the healthier we all will be?"

"I just found a quote: "Aspiring to awakening can awaken the deepest fear of all: discovering we do not exist in the way we think we do. . . . It makes us chronically restless and insecure. So we talk ourselves out of it; 'I can't do it;' 'I don't deserve it;' 'I'm tempting fate;' 'others won't understand;' 'I'll end up alone' (Angler, 1999, p. 2). "How did I get to live in this state of Ego? When does it develop?"

"The ego begins to form when we begin to define ourselves in relationship to others and by the roles we play in life and by identifying ourselves by words and labels outside ourselves. It is a form of recurring conditioned mental emotional thought patterns that identify it to form and attachment to something outside of itself. It is at this time that we begin to define ourselves with I am a scientist, a father, alcoholic, I am good, I am bad, I am stupid. We then begin to construct a sense of self based on the roles we play and identify with that representation as 'I.' Our early experiences are deeply rooted in our a sense of self as are our early mistaken beliefs and conclusions, such as "I am alone," or "I cannot trust my own perceptions." These beliefs continue to have a profound influence on our lives unless they are changed at the deepest levels of consciousness in our minds, bodies and emotions. These are roles that need to be retired.

Remember, we spoke about the roles you developed as a child with your mother, as the avoider, not to get her attention and with your father, as the clever information gatherer, to get his attention. These roles will play out with every woman you get into relationship with and you will never leave home unless you learn to let them go. So internally, you will either be always trying to find out "why" people act "that way" and persist doing so or try to avoid any feelings."

"Yes my past girlfriends said I would not let them get close to me! This is just what my mother used to say! I know I either want to track down answers but I also want to avoid feelings."

"We lose true wisdom as we learn rational intelligence. We learn as children that we need to "do" something to be safe and loved like be clever, wise, and aggressive as you were with your father, or, manipulative, distant, or quiet as you were with your mother. This is when the ego develops. Our roles have become overdeveloped and we forget who we really are. We get very busy "doing", and in order to let the ego go, we need to learn to take on new spontaneous roles and learn "role relief."

"As you talk about roles, I note that you are talking about something I am looking at about Jacob Levy Moreno. Do you know about him?"

Moreno (1889 - 1974) was a therapist who developed the action method of psychodrama and group psychotherapy. I use his techniques of psychodrama within the structure of the doors. We will talk more about this process and how it is so important later. In relation to what we are talking about now, it is important now is to understand that Moreno broke off from other traditional therapists such as Freud, stating that our personality is not hereditary but develops by the roles we learn to play in life. We are much more than the roles we play in life, in fact, the more roles we can learn to give up, the fewer roles we have to live up to, defend, or protect. We often remain stuck in these childhood roles because we feel that we are not enough and need to play a role, or need to "do" something in order to "get" recognition or love. As soon as we try to "be" something, we are focused on an outside goal and we construct a sense of self, and unite that sense of self into the 'I,' losing ourselves.

You are not your past. Sometimes it is difficult to let our old roles go for fear we will have no identity. We try to find ourselves in things outside of ourselves, such as material things, addictions; and then we lose ourselves in those things only to want more. This is one way that people can turn back from their spiritual path. We play roles to stay safe in childhood and remain stuck in these roles because we feel that we are not enough. The ego is shallow and short lived. Every time we have a new experience in this world, we have a chance to continue can changing our idea of our sense of self, or we can remain rigidly committed to our old roles denying ourselves our or sense of spontaneity."

"This sounds exhausting! So this is how come we have no gardens? Look what else I just found!"

I could see his delight in trying to please me just as he did with his father as a child when he took on the role of information gatherer.

"Joseph Campbell (1972) writes: "What is keeping us out of the garden [of Eden] is not the jealousy or wrath of any god, but our own instinctive attachment to what we take to be our lives. Our senses, outward-directed to the world of space and time, have attached us to that world and to our mortal bodies within it. We are loath to give up what we take to be the goods and pleasures of this physical life, and this attachment is the great fact, the great circumstance or barrier, that is keeping us out of the garden. This and this alone, is preventing us from recognizing within ourselves that immortal and universal consciousness of which our physical senses, outward turned, are but the agents" (p. 28).

"That is great Iye! Thank you. So it is important to note that this is how come we leave our spiritual path and allow our big fat ego to take over."

'My children say that I cannot be without a relationship, and that I lose myself when I am in one."

Addicted to Potential

"You may be what I call "Addicted to Potential"
    "That's a new one. What is that?"
    "Codependency, as I define it, (Miller, 2000), is an absence of relationship with the self. In order to feel safe in a dysfunctional or addictive family system, we begin to look outside ourselves for validation. When we are very young, we learn to attach to a parent who is not fully there for us and that attachment pattern becomes the role we play in order to get love. In the dysfunctional family system, love and attention are so inconsistent, that we become addicted to that inconsistency. Love means being addicted to waiting for the feelings of love that come from outside oneself; that is, we become *addicted to the potential of love.* We also become addicted to the potential of who that person could really be as well as to the inconsistency on our parents part. In relationships, the addiction becomes one of "Oh...who she could really be if she would just stop (drinking, using drugs, working, etc) because I saw who she could really be that one good time when she was there for me, and it felt so good"
    "I said that about my last wife because she worked all the time but every once and a while she would sit down and have dinner with me and I felt so wonderful. So I would pretend she really was not that way!"
    "Yes, we spend a lot of time waiting for that one good time and often we miss our own lives. Our addiction to potential begins in childhood. The worst abuse here is that the child becomes focused on the parent's development. In a healthy family system, the parents are focused on the child's development. Since codependency is an absence of relationship with the self, one is always seeking to attach to another person or thing and is always looking outside oneself for validation to learn how to act or feel. Soon, that insatiable hunger is almost always experienced as a desire for something else: For a relationship, for numbing the pain, for excitement, or other distractions from the pain, for material wealth and comfort, status and security, for a drink, a smoke, an orgasm, or for more pleasure or less pain (Miller. 2000).
    This addiction becomes one of potential because one never can find the perfect other. In addictive relationships, it is about who the other person could be. If we become addicted to our own potential, instead of moving forward, we engage in self-sabotaging behavior. We learn that in order to "be" or to exist, we must first "do" something, in

order to "get" love. Often, that is why I call an addiction a spiritual calling, but one that goes to the wrong address.

A child who is worried about their parents and dissociates from their own needs will focus on "What is missing – what might have been – what never can be." They become codependent and can become aggressive by idealizing their past and remembering that "one good time" and feel bitter resentment at its having been taken away. This child experiences deep loss of self-confidence and an apprehension about attempting to overcome the loss. Often, he tries to recreate the situation or that one good time but with the wrong people."

"In my case over and over again! Relationship after relationship!"

"We attach or bond to a parent with one or a combination of the following patterns: victim, aggressor, or passive-aggressive. Whatever the pattern, the child sacrifices connection with the self to maintain this "connection" or bond with our primary caregivers as love (Miller, 2000). Any of these choices leaves the child paralyzed with psychic deadness and a loss of meaning, alienated, estranged, and facing the eradication of her identity (Eigen, 1992). The true self retreats to a zone of safety but it is shell-shocked, made into an object (Spiegel, 1997), unreal even to herself.

Separation from the family is difficult for this child because he/she is worried for its own safety and security. Often, he/she cannot complete this necessary stage of separation. If one is always focused on what one needs to survive in a family, one cannot focus on one's own personal development. Spontaneity, creativity, and openness – attributes of the spiritual self- are barely perceptible. This addiction to potential is difficult to break since it is experienced internally as the source of self-love and later becomes the cause of self-defeating behavior (Miller, 2000). When love and attention are shown in this family system, it is often negative and associated with abuse. Codependents believe they are not allowed to have, or do not deserve to have, sufficient love, or to experience it too long. They are actually frightened when experiencing intimacy. Teaching intimacy can only be accomplished in a consistent loving atmosphere or, if the clients are advanced enough, within the framework of a regular group which imitates the dynamics of a healthy family system. Dysfunctional roles tend to exist for sometime even after they have outlived their usefulness. These roles remain stubbornly functional. The client from this population is often fiercely loyal but mainly only to the dysfunction of the family. Never having had an identity, their dysfunction becomes their identity. The adult is often reluctant to give up their old "label" even after many years of counseling. Their diagnosis becomes their reality and their lifestyle." (Miller, 2000)

"In AA I got a label as an alcoholic and it felt good. I finally had some identity."

"Yes, but you are much more than a label."

If Only Syndrome

"When I was a boy I used to think "Wow who I could really be if I could invent something wonderful. Then my father would notice me and love me."

"This is a good example of how this addiction to potential stops one from feeling true self-love. We become addicted to our own potential of who we could be. "If only"…if only I had more money, if only I was better looking…if only I was smarter, if only I had all the answers, then I would be loved. The child whose attachment style is avoidant will focus on doing what I he has to do, appear to tolerate many things, and will deal with things on his own. He will dismiss or discount the value of what has been lost within the family and inflate a positive self image often becoming the "golden child.""

"That sounds like me. I just began to feel anxious as a child and that continues today."

"When there is inconsistency and disorganization within the structure in a family such as yours, you may have separated from your soul as a defense to "be loved", became highly anxious about what was missing in your family, and at the same time, became very fearful to talk about talking about it. You became addicted to the inconsistency within the family."

"We could never talk about feelings, only facts in our family." Iye said sadly.

"Yes, for the ego ignorance is bliss. The ego loves to ignore the truth. This ignorance is an active not wanting to know, a resistance to knowing. This is more comfortable sometimes as no one has to change! The ego thinks that things like anxiety, self-doubt, and fear of not succeeding, of not getting what we want, of failing to live up to our ambitions and ideals, fear of looking deeply into ourselves will keep us safe and give us freedom. The ego loves to put down our aspirations especially the more noble and ambitious they are eliciting secret shame or guilt in ourselves or the fear of envy or ridicule from others."

Putting the Ego on a Diet

"Here is something from Maslow that sounds just like something along the line you said."

"Again, I am glad you are doing the research, Iye. I can see how come you are so good at it." Iye looked proud.

"Maslow said (1968, p. 33), "What we take to be our 'self' and feel to be so present and real is actually an internalized image, a composite representation, constructed by a selective and imaginative 'remembering' of past encounters with the object world. In fact, the self is viewed as being constructed a new from moment to moment."

"Our early childhood experiences are deeply embedded and very basic in our construction of a sense of self and the early mistaken beliefs and conclusions, such as "I am bad," or "I am alone," or "I cannot trust my own perceptions," continue to have a very deep influence on our choices for our life until they are changed cognitively, somatically, emotionally. We deny ourselves spontaneity, choosing experiences which will validate our pre constructed beliefs and thus we remain rigidly committed to our old roles. We remain in old roles and patterns of behavior and we don't know what to do with certain new stimuli or learning. To become balanced, the individual's Self must transform the ego and achieve alignment with its individuality (Eddinger, 1972; Jung & von Franz, 1964). However, the ego fears the loss of what is known "its identity" and resists by struggling with the unknown aspect of self."

Iye: *"This sounds like somehow we would rather be right than happy! Or fat than happy?"*

"Yes, if we drop the "I" in our false identity, our rational intelligence, we will allow ourselves to have new experiences in this world, and will allow our sense of self to be constructed new from moment to moment."

"How can the ego surrender? Who or what am I surrendering to?"

"To something more loving and higher than yourself. When we do the work needed to do to surrender and let go, there is a transformation. Any transformational process takes work and often we want any easy answer. If you want the ego to get thinner, you will have to let go of the beliefs that you are alone, or that you are engulfed, that you are worthless, stupid, or that people around you are incompetent, that you are helpless and powerless, or that you are able to keep yourself safe by controlling everything within your experience. In other words, you will have to give up control. When we become bored, feeling isolated, separated, desperate, this is a great time to begin your spiritual journey and reconnect with the soul. Living on purpose does involve a death of the old roles we have played and the old beliefs we have held of who we are. Many people are afraid to take the action to move forward to become who they truly are for it will involve suffering in letting go of who they thought they were, identified by labels outside of themselves that are ego based that keep us disconnected from God. How do you label yourself? How do you label others? Be aware that any label is limiting. Labels stick us in a box where there's no room to move.

When we live in the land of ego, we tend to think that every problem requires an explanation in order for it to be resolved: however, the search for explanations severely limits a person's forward movement. This is especially true if you believe that explanations need to be difficult and problematic. If we keep getting our energy from problems, we will keep creating problems to experience energy, and severely limit our thinking and creativity. This feeds the ego and stops one from living in the present and tuned into the moment."

"So we need to put the ego on a diet?"

"That is a great analogy Iye. It's the ego that needs the diet or the rational IQ -not the body so to speak."

"Yes, I know lots of thin people with big egos!"

"One of my associates, Adam Blatner said that role playing helps one to let go and surrender their point of view that the ego holds and through role reversal, to open imaginatively to the perspective of the other and it also helps to consolidate a deeper identity in which one is capable of feeling comfortable in "being wrong." Role playing achieves this through the repeated exercise of spontaneity, because improvisation will lead a person to discover that the subconscious can be a great source of wisdom, inspiration, and creativity."

"Let me look him up. What is a healthy ego?"

"Important indications of mental health, of a healthy Ego, are the ability to distinguish between the outer world and the inner world of wishes and impulses, and the ability to distinguish between 'self' and 'not self,' or what is under one's control and what is not under one's control. When we stop playing roles we become can become fully present and focused on the situation and become the natural spontaneous person we are meant to be. Souldrama teaches us how to release the old roles in our lives and practice taking on new ones in action. It allows the ego to get thinner in order to see our divine selves."

"Wow, I have a lot of weight to lose."

"We all do. This is a very overweight country. Now is a good time to talk about soul."

"Why aren't you happy? It's because ninety-nine percent of everything you do, and think, and say, is for yourself -- and there isn't one."

- Wu Wei Wu-

Chapter Three

> *My soul is the bridge between spirit and body and, as such,*
> *is a uniter of opposites. ...Without soul at center, I would*
> *either transcend into spirit or become mired in matter."*
> *-Marion Woodman-*

The Role of the Soul

Iye asked: *"What is the soul? What defines spirit? How do we define Soul?"*

"Slow down, Iye. This is another attempt to define something. The soul (Greek work psyche) is an essential part of every one of us, as is a difficult challenge to know the soul with the conscious mind is for it exists in the realm of the invisible. Every time we attempt to define something, we feed the ego as it opens us up to comparisons and judgments, so it is difficult to define the word with the everyday mind.

In fact, Thomas Moore states that "The soul has its own set of rules, which are not the same as those of life. Unlike the steady progress of history, for instance, the events of the soul are cyclic and repetitive. Familiar themes come round and round. The past is more important than the future. The living and the dead have equal roles. Emotions and the sense of meaning are paramount. Pleasures are deep, and pain can reach the very foundations of our existence. The soul doesn't evolve or grow; it cycles and twists repeats and reprises, echoing ancient themes common to all human beings. It is always circling home. Gnostic tales tell of the homesickness of the soul, its yearning for its own milieu, which is not this world of fact. Its odyssey is a drifting at sea, a floating toward home, not an evolution toward perfection. (Moore, 1998)"

"Wow, this is really heavy!"

"When we label something, and define ourselves in relation to something outside of ourselves, it opens us up to judgments and comparisons from others as to who has the best definition. This is what makes it heavy. But to go on, the soul needs relationship. Simpkinson & Simpkinson, (1998), refer to the fact that we occupy a fixed place in our families, in a location on the earth, in creation. The soul has a "rightful place" and exists in relationship with everything else. The soul's essence is therefore connectedness; it thrives on relationship.

Throughout the world, many of the major philosophies speak of the relationship between soul and breath making the transition from 'breath' to 'spirit' (Eliade, 1977, p. 178). I love what Hillman says (1975)," The soul is one's grand scheme of relationships: one "can never grasp it apart from other things, perhaps because it is like a reflection in a flowing mirror, or like the moon which mediates only borrowed light. "

"Can we see the soul? Where is it? How do I know my soul is here? I cannot see it."

"Do you see the wind Iye?"

"No."

"How do you know it is there?"

"I feel it. I see its effects. Oh, I get it."

"Like the wind, that refines, purifies, and transforms, when we connect to the soul, we feel love and compassion, inner joy, and happiness. If we believe that the soul is based in the heart, then connecting with it opens one to an inner source of love and compassion. We can connect to a source of inner joy and happiness that is intrinsic, no matter what is going on outside of us, we will feel grounded within no matter what we will face in life's circumstances. Connecting to the soul brings a deep sense of presence and peace within yourself while at the same time you will feel an intuitive interconnectedness with all other beings and nature. You will have a spontaneous empathy for others, an ability to understand those around us more deeply, or as Moreno said "To see ourselves through another's eyes." You will know when that happens. The "soul emergence," or the increasing connection to one's soul, may be recognized by the development of presence, love, joy, peace, and empathy, and the diminishing of fear. " (Cortright, 1997, p.136)

The soul is the place where god-energy flows (Schwartz, 1999). The language of the soul is vision and not words. One way to envision the soul is as the positive luminous energy field that surrounds us or as one's spiritual identity. Today, we tend to think of soul as a deep inner world, a space within a person, separate from the body, from the personality, from the mind, and detached from the community and from concerns of the world."

"So it's like the body is a parking garage for the soul?"

"I love how you are beginning to think creatively."

Will the Real Me Please Stand Up?

"Is there a difference between sprit and soul?'

"I do not want to get caught up here in definitions; however, Jung (1933), Hillman (1978), and Moore (1992) describe spirit as descending from above seeking unity and harmony whereas soul comes from that within us and ascends from the depths of our being."

"How do I experience the soul? How do I know when I've found my soul?"

"You have never really "lost" your soul but have become disconnected from it. The challenge is to put the ego and soul into alignment so that the two can establish a relationship."

"How did I become disconnected?"

"Jung (1959) talks about this and refers to the lessening of the personality as "loss of soul" (p. 119). When we experience early childhood trauma, Jung said that "soul moves at the weak point where the personality is thin, where things are not secure and stable. That's where soul has an entry" (as cited in Moore, 1998, p. 45).

"So in other words, you can say that if our ego is too fat, the soul cannot enter".

"That is one way to put it. Go back to when you were a child and something frightened you. You can probably remember saying "I held my breath". This could have been when you held your breath and disconnected with the soul, and lost your spontaneity, will, passion, integrity, and life force, in order to survive and stay safe. It was then that we redefined ourselves as wounded and abandoned and banished the soul in order to survive, making the ego fatter and fatter. The soul must accept the felt sense of a divided self or as Eiseman (1989) refers "It becomes a Spirit in Exile" (p. 13). This is when we begin to develop defenses against the pain of being hurt or violated and our true self or soul goes into hiding. Thomas Moore (1992, p.xi) says, "The great malady of the twentieth century, implicated in all of our troubles and affecting us individually and socially, is 'loss of soul'

"Wow, this is sad."

"Yes, and time to lighten up. Let's talk about our spiritual journey!"

Chapter Four

> *When you are able to contain both the light and dark together, that is a very enlightening state. It means that you no longer have to choose one experience over another. You do not have to choose love or hate, blame or forgiveness, sadness or joy, anger or openheartedness. You are no longer polarized; no particular feeling boxes you in and keeps you from the light of true self. You then have access to the full range of human experiences you came into this life to embrace.*
>
> *- M. Nelson-*

Our Spiritual Journey

As we continued our walk and arrived at the library, Iye kept talking: *"I understand Souldrama to be like a spiritual journey. What is the difference between spirituality and religion and what really is a spiritual journey?"*

"This is a big question. Let's see if I can answer this! To me a true spiritual path is simply removing the obstructions of who we truly are. I define spirituality as a personal relationship to the divine presence that dwells within us and in all things. I choose to call that presence God. You may choose to call that presence by some other name such as Higher Power, etc. The more we can explore our relationship with this presence, the more we can search for our higher potential. There are many paths to this "Presence" or divinity. To experience divinity is a simple thing as divinity is everywhere.

The more we can explore our relationship with the divine, the more we can search for our higher potential. We all have the capacity for creativity, for love, justice, for searching for wisdom and beauty. We need to simplify our consciousness to experience the divine in all things, to return home and back to our spiritual intelligence.

People often view the spiritual path as a search for the light. In truth, spirituality asks us to bring light and darkness together in wholeness. And in fact, this is the only possible solution. In our world of duality, any effort to focus all attention on the light only serves to increase the power of the darkness. Our aim is not to deny or reject anything but to embrace it all."

"So this is like religion? If I become spiritual, will I be going against my religion?"

"Not at all. Many people get confused between the words spirituality and religion. The word 'religion' comes from roots which mean to 'tie together,' that the spiritual involves not only faith, prayer, and values, but also obligations to and support from others (Miller, 2007). Religion is the practice of spirituality. Religion seems to be a set of thoughts or beliefs. People who choose to identify with these beliefs choose to practice this religion. It is important not to make these beliefs our identity. Our beliefs do not make us a spiritual person nor does the church or people there with whom you associate. In fact, the more we make our beliefs our identity, the more we become cut off from our spirituality because it is then that we begin to define ourselves by our religious beliefs, causing us to become more ego identified. The mind takes over and says that we need to think as "they "do. This is where we begin to judge ourselves and others by comparing our religions to others. Religions can bring separation and spirituality brings unity. Remember, an absence of spirituality reflects itself when one feels separate from others. There is no "my religion is better than yours" and no comparisons. We are all one."

"So we are all one no matter what religion we practice? I have not gone to church in years!"

"Exactly. There are many religions in the world and many different paths. Many different religions practice spirituality and religion is meant to make us feel closer to God not more separate. Every time we separate ourselves from God, we are separating ourselves from God's vision of love and our own loving hearts. Follow your own path is my ultimate advice but remember what ever path you choose to follow in the end, we all want one thing and that is to be loved."

"I am scared to let go and change and perhaps I am using my religion as an excuse."

"This is good insight, Iye. The question arises how do we go past the fear, delusion, and need for power which causes so much personal conflict in relationships within us and between others? Fear, greed, and power come from the ego's need to attach itself to something outside itself to obtain recognition and identity. Religion is about having a set of rules that come from the outside of yourself-not the inside. It does not mean that some of these rules are not good, but that change needs to come from the life and love inside of you. We can know all the right answers and what to say and what the Bible says we should say, but not know God at all."

"Rules and answers are much simpler than relationships."

"That is true; Iye, but they can't love you back."

Say Ahhhh!

"Did you know Iye, that there are over one thousand words for the word "God" and they all have the "Ahhh sound" to them?"

"Wow, like Judah and Buddha, Allah?"

"Yes, call that divine presence whatever you want. Whatever you name your Higher Power, the most important thing is that it is loving. Those who love God come from every system that exists and every institution. Their love is part of their transformation. It is important to stay connected to that divine presence within you."

"When it comes to our spiritual journey, who can I trust to help guide me?"

"There are many authorities, mentors, priests, pastors, and many religions, Christian, Hebrew, Muslim, and Buddhist. In the end, it is our own relationship to our higher power, our ultimate source of being that counts. What matters is how we can really own that spiritual relationship, internalize it, empower ourselves, and become part of the healing creative power of the universe."

"There must be some research about this that I can look up." said Iye.

(This is where I got impatient again and I knew that this is where I needed to learn tolerance for others on my own journey.) I realized that Iye's fear of changing was so great that he needed the comfort of words. I continued with my challenge.

"Many authors provide a common thread to define a spiritual journey (Covey, 1989; Mitroff, 1994; Morris, 1997; Neal, 1997; Peck, 1993; Roof, 1993; Stein & Hollwitz, 1992). In general, they refer to the spiritual journey as a process of focusing within, in order to gain an awareness of self. Only through this awareness of self can individuals become truly actualized and find meaning and purpose in their work and in their lives. This is the individuation process that produces both an interconnection with self and a connection with others by fostering a sense of order and balance (Miller 2007)."

"Again this is about relationships."
"Yes."

Living in the Light

"So that means I need to find my own truth of whom I really am independently from the opinion of others-even in a relationship? I can stop defining myself s an alcoholic?"

"Yes, but to go on. Chandler et al. (1992) has a good definition. He describes the spiritual experience as the innate ability to transcend the point of view of the ego from which people constantly experience and evaluate and judge their lives. When they can do this, they can open up to a broader worldview, a greater capacity for loving, and an increased motivation to enhance the greater good. Elkins and associates (1988) offers another definition of spirituality : Spirituality, which comes from the Latin *spiritus*, meaning "breath of life," is a way of being and experiencing that comes about through awareness of a transcendent dimension and is characterized by certain identifiable values in regard to self, others, nature, life, and whatever one considers to be the Ultimate (p. 10). In 1988, they go on to define the common elements people experience during a spiritual journey: transcendence, personal meaning and mission in life, sacredness, and material values, altruism, and high ideals, awareness of the tragic, and fruits of spirituality."

"Can you expand on them?"

(1)   "Let's talk about the *transcendent dimension.* The spiritual person believes that there is an inspirational dimension to life and that there is in an "unseen world" that contact with is beneficial. They may have the traditional view of a personal God to a psychological view that the "transcendent dimension" is simply a natural extension of the conscious self into the regions of the unconscious. The spiritual person is one who has had what Maslow referred to as "peak experiences and he or she draws personal power through contact with this dimension. (Keutzer, 1978; Laski, 1961; Wuthnow, 1978;) offer the "triggers" and effects of transcendent or "peak" experiences The spiritual person believes that what they see is not all that there is."

"So what I see is not what I get?"
"Exactly, now to go on.

(2) *Meaning and purpose in life.* Even though the meaning varies for each person, there exists a common factor that each person has a sense that their life has meaning and purpose, and has known the spiritual journey.

(3) *Mission in life.* The spiritual person feels a sense of responsibility to life, a calling to answer, a mission to accomplish, or in some cases, even a destiny to fulfill this mission. He or she develops a passion to discover this mission and understands that in "losing one's life" one "finds it."

(4) *Sacredness of life.* The spiritual person believes life is infused with sacredness and often experiences a sense of awe, reverence, and wonder even in "nonreligious" settings. There are no polarities such love and hate but believes all of life is "holy" and that the sacred is in the ordinary. There is a sense of oneness and all of life is sacred."

"Does this mean I have to give up money and be poor? Are spiritual people poor?"

"Let me go on, Iye. I was just getting to that. (Now, I could see what made Iye anxious.)

(5) *Material values.* The spiritual person appreciates material goods and possessions, but does not see these things as something outside of themselves that gives them satisfaction, but as a tool to help them and others fulfill their own spiritual mission. They do not use them as a substitute for frustrated spiritual needs.

(6) *Altruism.* The spiritual person has a sense of a universal intelligence. The spiritual person is touched by the pain and suffering of others. He or she has a strong sense of social justice and is committed to altruistic love and action. The spiritual person knows that "no man is an island" and that we are all "part of the continent" of common humanity. On a round world and there are no sides.

(7) *Idealism.* The spiritual person is a visionary committed to the betterment of the world. He or she loves things for what they are; yet' also for what they can become. The spiritual person is committed to high ideals and to the realization of positive potential in all aspects of life."

"Like Mother Theresa?"

I nodded.

(8) *Awareness of the tragic.* The spiritual person is conscious of the tragic realities of human existence and is deeply aware of human pain, suffering, and death. This awareness gives depth to the spiritual person and provides him or her with an existential seriousness toward life. This in itself helps the person's joy, appreciation, and valuing of life.

(9) *Fruits of spirituality.* The spiritual person is one whose spirituality has made a difference in his or her life. True spirituality made a difference upon one's relationship to self, others, nature, life, and whatever one considers being the Ultimate (pp. 10-12)."

"I guess what you are saying then make sense. So how do I become a spiritual person?"

"If we begin to believe that we have a life separate from God, we will begin to have painful experiences that are disconnected from God and we will believe that we can "control" our life. I believe that our spiritual work is to help others believe that they do not have two lives- a life with God and then another life without God.--all our spiritual work is to help break down the idea that we are separate from God. It is important to do this work because without an awareness of what we are, our unique patterns of God within each individual, also known as our life's purpose, will not be expressed. We all have that unique dimension within us that a god is expressed through and within us. We can obtain many riches emotionally, spiritually, and materialistically but without spiritual maturity we will feel whole but as though "something is missing".

"So that is what living in the light means?"

"Exactly. You can become a spiritual seeker or a disciple. A seeker keeps reading the right books and stores the knowledge. Nothing stops a disciple until they wake up and that means doing the work necessary to see what is blocking their path to hear God's message. Nothing will stop their intent- they will take the courses and do the workshops so that they can create an atmosphere where that will happen. Their inner voice will speak to them and tell them to do the work. They are committed to the path.

So when we desire to take a spiritual path, we need also to look at our motivation to do so. If we do so from the level of the ego, then we are still holding on to the ego and are afraid to truly afraid to "let go". The deeper path is for connection with God on the level of soul, returning to one's created existence and surrendering one's will and identity to God's. I prefer the latter way."

Sink the Titanic

"So Iye, (I was getting anxious to move forward but had to remind myself where I was), you invited me here to do the Souldrama workshop. Let's begin to take action!"

"Wow, this is a lot to accomplish. Maybe I am not ready. Maybe I should get all my things in order before I begin."

"I often tell my clients to line up the deck chairs on the Titanic before it sinks. Don't wait to begin your spiritual journey until you have enough money, the right, home, or for life's circumstances to be right. Begin your journey now and you can begin to be a co-creator in your own life and begin to make the changes you need to be on your higher purpose. Don't wait or you will miss your own life. Don't wait or you will miss that relationship you have been dreaming about."

"That is motivation right there! How will I know that I am on the right path?"

"You will know that for yourself when you begin. A word of warning for when you begin this path, don't get caught up in the question of how am I doing? What we are experiencing never needs to be analyzed. If we wonder if we have forgiven someone, we have not, if we wonder if we are feeling the peace of God, we are not. Only the ego judges one day's peace with another's. As you are journeying along your spiritual path, remember not to compare one day's journey with the next or you will be again measuring, comparing, and judging your progress and feeding the ego."

"I do want to be loved Iye said with a tear in his eye. I am ready to take action, but before we do, can you talk more about the Ego and the Soul? I like this".

"I want to share a passage from Martia Nelson's book, 'Coming Home' (1995): "My greatest teacher was the experience of living in split realities: personality and true self. Personality is our daily companion, our conscious self that sees the world through the eyes of limitation and dutifully keeps us informed about what we can and cannot do. True self, on the other hand, patiently stands by, offering the unwavering knowledge that a state of vibrant well-being and unlimited possibility is our true nature, a birthright that can be lived if we choose to do so. True self simply refers to the aspect of our being that is completely aware of its expanded nature no matter what we may be experiencing at the time.

Whenever we feel constrained, fearful, unworthy, and inadequate or anything we deem to be negative, we have identified with our personality. We can always choose to view the same situation from the perspective of our soul."

"Let's move on to the second floor of the library and I will show you the model for Souldrama .Maybe this will help. Then we can talk about the ego and the soul, and you can do your own research."

"Let's Go!"

Chapter Five

> *"The consensus of Kabalistic opinion regards the mystical way to God as a reversal of the process by which we have emanated from God. To know the stages of the creative process is also to know the stages of one's own return to the root of all existence." –Shoham-*

Aligning the Ego and the Soul

"So why do we want to align the ego and soul?"

"Let's sit down now and look up some research before we begin the workshop tomorrow." This made Iye happy.

"Everything in our life happens in relationship and that includes the relationship between the ego and soul. By growing spiritually, we can begin to reconnect with our true spiritual identity by realigning and repairing the separation between ego and soul. Through this process, we are really dissolving the strength of the ego and aligning it with the soul and reconnecting to intimate relationships. We are not eliminating the ego. If we repair the bond with our souls following disconnection, we will be able to grow spiritually. Notice how your disappointment and frustration eventually became a catalyst for movement and change."

"Don't remind me."

"We can learn to trust this natural, unfolding process. Moments of shame and trauma in childhood affected our development, and we sacrificed parts of ourselves in order to feel safe or loved (Zimberoff & Hartman, 2007). Inner resources such as innocence, trust, spontaneity, courage, and self-esteem were lost, stolen, or abandoned, leaving an immense empty space (Miller, 2007) or that hole in the soul. Spiritual growth is achieved through the repair of the bond with our soul following disconnection (Zimberoff & Hartman, 1999). Strength of character, resilience, determination, and deep trust all come from repair and realignment of the separation between the ego and soul. This repair results from the authentic relationships we form with others and from the risks we take and our willingness to change our roles in relationship to them.

When you are challenged to grow and change such as you have been, Iye, your relationships can be an appeal for your soul to awaken and reconnect to the ego. Soul, according to Hillman (1978), is most apt to emerge in those chaotic, 'pathological' moments when we experience the disintegration of our beliefs, values, and security, for it is in such moments that our imagery, emotions, desires, and values are heightened and we have the fullest awareness of the psyche in its essential form. Indeed, for Hillman, the very point of deconstructing our fixed ideas in psychology is paradoxically to provide us with the conditions for the revelation of psyche itself. (As cited in Drob, 1999, p. 58)."

"You have made a good point. Decker (1993) says "Trauma acts to increase spiritual development if that development is defined as an increase in the search for purpose and meaning" (p.33). Iye beaming said; here are some more facts that I found in one of the books on the library shelf.

Carl Jung's theory of individuation states that the individual strives to become whole and distinctive from the collective (Jung, 1933; Jung & von Franz, 1964). In order for an individual to realize their specific purpose, connection with one's unique self must be achieved (Eddinger, 1972; Harding, 1965). In this context, self is the whole of the individual, including all aspects of an individual's conscious and unconscious, often referred to as a paradoxical union of opposites (Harding, 1965). The Self is superior to the ego and is experienced as the center of the personality (Jung, 1933). Although the path to individuation is quite different for each person, the process tends to be similar (Singer, 1972). If individuals become conscious of their whole personality, the self, they can become great spiritual leaders by becoming aware of their higher purposes and potential capabilities. The individuation process occurs as one's ego is initially developed, then challenged, and ultimately subordinated to a more comprehensive psychic entity, the Self (Jung, 1933; Singer, 1972). The process constitutes the conscious realization and fulfillment of one's unique being (Harding, 1965)."

"Great research! Regarding the self and ego, Carl Jung believed the self to be the "being" mode, representing the feminine principle and the ego as representing the "doing," the masculine principle, (Weisstub, 1997). When the two become aligned, it is then that we have a balance between the conscious and unconscious ways of operating and can achieve the goal of self-actualization or individuation. Jung (1958) named this the "transcendent function."

"Hmm... so, this is where, intellect and intuition become balanced in relationship to one another. Being and doing become balanced," he proudly declared.

"Look at how you identified with your mother growing up. The mother's function, at the highest level, is to create an environment for her baby in which it is safe to be nobody. Winnicott considered it vital in healthy development for the child to be allowed periods of time in unstructured states of being that he called "going-on-being" (as cited in Greenberg & Mitchell, 1983). "The mother's non demanding presence makes the experience of formlessness and comfortable solitude possible, and this capacity becomes a central feature in the development of a stable and personal self" (p. 193). In a state free of anxiety, each person is content to be alone without being withdrawn. Each person, totally secure in the availability of the other, has no need for active contact. There is no sense of aloneness, or of intrusion. Each individual is momentarily undefended and at peace. This is an example of attachment and detachment or connection and separation of the natural relationship we have between our own ego and soul. When we begin to stand and walk as children, we are finally ready to "let go." In the same way, only when our ego is solid are we prepared to move beyond the realm of "I am what I can do," to transcend the normal, to let go of the known and to venture into a wholly new level of self-exploration."

"I wish my mother had left me alone sometimes. This means we all should have done this separation at age two and not now. No wonder I have a problem. I did not want to attach to my mother! I felt smothered."

(I let Iye go on to satisfy his own ego and because research was his forte and he was on a roll! He continued.)

"We have been talking about connection and relatedness. Maslow (1987) said that self-actualizing men and women are able to transcend an inadequate environment "because of the ability of healthy people to be detached from their surroundings, which is the same as saying that they live by their inner laws rather than by outer pressures" (p. 121). Wow, is this really possible? If I do not do this workshop, will I reconnect with my own soul?"

"I don't know. However, I do know that this process will help you move forward in this lifetime to remove the barriers where you are stuck. The ego and soul and can begin to begin again to be intimate relationship with each other, their alignment can result in strength of character, resilience, determination, and deep trust. I believe we can help people grow spiritually through realigning the ego and soul through the process of Souldrama. This is not a religious process but merely a group action method to align our egos and soul to reconnect those parts of ourselves that we sacrificed."

Don't Reject the Ego

"I guess that answers my question. Do I need to get rid of the ego?"

"Not at all. Don't reject the ego. Again, what we really want is that the ego forms a relationship with the soul and works as a partner or co-creator forgetting the "I" and changing it to a "we". We do not want the ego to dissolve but to surrender. For like you, if you lost all your weight, you would be invisible. Many people in therapy must first undergo a process of ego-strengthening before they are ready to become who they truly are, to accept their shadow parts, to open up or even begin to let go of, the ego's limited, idealized self-concept. It is important that an individual have a "healthy ego" before they begin this work for so that a person is able to absorb and integrate transpersonal experiences and not be overpowered by them."

"So on the other hand, it makes sense that before I get into another relationship, I put my ego on a diet and surrender my will so that I can see this woman when she appears".

"When the ego begins to get "thinner" and you can recognize that truth of who you really are your second phase of life can begin."

"So there is more in life?"

"Yes, Iye, much more. Remember, I used to live in this land of Ego. However, the first phase must be completed or the second phase will not succeed. In other words, the ego of the spiritual seeker must be so strong and healthy so that it dis-identifies from the many fragmented selves and surrenders itself to a higher purpose than its own self-interest."

"So it's like not too much ego or too little but just enough. This reminds me of the story of three bears."

"I did not know you read fairy tales."

"I did as a child. When I would go to my room alone, I read everything I could so I would not miss anything. Words were my friends."

"It looks like you still do."

"Look at this article I found (Block & Block, 1980). People with high ego-control are rigid and inhibited, disposed to repress impulses and emotions, to feel anxious in new situations, and to reject unexpected information. Those who have weak ego-control are impulsive and distractible, and do not have the discipline to concentrate on one task for very long. The synthesis of these two polar extremes is not moderate ego-control, but rather "ego resiliency." Ego resiliency is the ability to respond flexibly but also persistently to challenges."

"All that reading paid off! Thank you! The ego must be in a unified, complete conscious state for transformation to occur. Jung said that later in midlife, the ego has a tendency to undergo a reversal of the "I-Thou" dualistic ego. "The first half of which is devoted to ego development and the second half of which is devoted to a return of the ego to its underlying source in the collective unconscious or objective psyche" (Washburn, 1995, p. 21).

"The spiritual journey unfolds through two stages, the path of the ego or personality where we are born as individuals in the world of form and in this physical world experience separation and limitation. The second path is that of the soul that takes us home again when we have experienced enough pain. This is where we let go of the illusion of separation to embrace unity and wholeness. It is only with a strong and healthy personality that we become capable of expressing soul. It is important that we ask ourselves where we are on our path."

"I feel like running, said Iye. I don't know if I have the energy to begin this process. I feel depleted and yet a bundle of anxiety!"

"Perhaps your own ego and intellect are beginning to feel challenged. When we are off a spiritual path, we can feel a depletion of energy. All healing is meant to increase our energy and connection to life. Jung (1959) talked about the "loss of soul" or a diminished energy in primitive psychology (p. 119). We all have at sometime experienced the inability to use energy effectively, because of ignorance or because of conflicting emotions; such as fear, rage, depression, or simply lack of motivation. Csikszentmihalyi (1993) suggests that the most common cause of lack of energy in life is the preoccupation with concerns about the self, worries about how we look or whether others like us or not, in other words, self-consciousness *(p. 185).*One of the purposes of Souldrama is to reduce the anxiety in our lives. The doors in Souldrama can be related to the seven basic situations of anxiety the Buddhists called Dukkha."

"I have heard of the Buddha when I studied religion and philosophy!"

"Let's look up what he said about a healthy way of living." (This I knew would keep Iye busy)

"Yes, the Buddha recommends a healthy way of living. He said that one of the functions of a healthy and well integrated ego is to align our thinking and living in harmony with reality! Boy I am really sick. I love to fanaticize!"

"Try not to be so hard on yourself, Iye. Important signs of a healthy Ego are the ability to distinguish between the outer world and the inner world of wishes and impulses, and the ability to distinguish between 'self' and 'not self,' or what is under one's control and what is not under one's control."

"You mean like when I keep dreaming about the girl who is waiting for me?"

"Yes. The Buddha believed that the basic problem of anxiety is experienced in relation to seven basic situations: 1) birth, 2) old age, 3) disease, 4) death, 5) meeting unpleasant people and circumstances, 6) parting from pleasant people and circumstances, 7) frustration of desire. The Buddha sees our self image as a bundle of anxiety, which is the sum total of the identification with all worries, anxieties, fears and feelings of insecurity, which are basic to life. The ultimate purpose of Buddhism is to produce an individual who is free from the emotional experience of the self...or one who can let go of the "I." The ego experiences this identification with the "I" as the feeling of power."

"I have experienced all of these! Wow! I should be a bundle of anxiety!"

I just glanced at him.

Iye looked down at his feet. "I always worry about what others think."

"This is natural. If you have experienced trauma as a child, your ego will be stronger than a child who is secure. You will keep holding onto your ego and it will keep you further removed the connection with your soul."

"Well I guess something is better than nothing if that is all I thought I had in my life."

Help! I Can't Let Go

"Yes and we hold on to that "something". Self-esteem is not reinforced by trauma but instead, trauma reinforces the ego and all the defense mechanisms and roles that ego comes to identify as self. Chögyam Trungpa (2005) relates that "at a certain stage the defense mechanisms you have set up become more powerful than you are. When you become used to the overwhelming quality of the defense mechanisms, when, for a moment, they are absent, you feel very insecure" (p. 109). The ego holds on and cannot conceive of letting go its grasp."

"In other words, we are afraid to let go?"

"Yes, and just a note about control. "'Enlightenment' has been likened to an open hand. When you try to grasp it, you transform your open hand into a fist. The very attempt to possess it (the action mode) banishes the state because it is a function of the receptive mode" (Deikman, 1980, p. 267). So it is with the ego's connection with the soul: efforts to protect it, based on early traumatic responses drive out the connection using our rational intelligence."

"So the more I try to control the ego, the tighter it holds on. This sounds very tiring! So it sounds like the ego ultimately wants to know that the divine is in control?"

"It sounds that way. Usually it takes some form of encouragement, support, connections with outside groups to help us let go of old beliefs and roles, help us to begin to see our higher purpose and access our spiritual intelligence. Csikszentmihalyi (1993) said that "To avoid psychic entropy from taking over consciousness, to maintain the gains our ancestors have made, while increasing psychic complexity for the use of our descendants, it is necessary to take part in activities that are themselves differentiated and integrated." (p. 170-171)

"So now I am working for my ancestors also?"

"Yes, actually the work you are about to do will help three generations back and three forward."

"I do hope to help my children by letting them see me be healthy and in a good relationship. How did you ever discover all of this?"

"Let's walk over to the group room where I can set up the chart that defines the stages of Souldrama." (I wanted to bring Iye into the world of visualization).

" Look what else I found! (I practiced patience) In the words of Washburn (1990,): "self-transcendence or salvation is achieved by a reunion of the self with its ground. The "sinful" or falsely autonomous

self must undergo a "conversion" and, then, reconciliation with its spiritual source. The "fallen" self must quit its self-defeating self-assertion and submit itself to the higher power it has denied, reestablishing thereby a connection that is vital to the self's integrity and well-being. This reconnection redeems the self and leads to a higher wholeness in which the self, fully developed and self-responsible, is a faithful instrument of its ground. The self is in this way "justified," "saved," "wedded," or otherwise rendered right in its relationship with its source. The broken essential relationship is restored on a higher plane." (p. 13).

"So I am marrying my own soul? I thought I was looking for a woman!"

"We'll see."

> *"Unity consciousness is a state of enlightenment where we pierce the mask of illusion which creates separation and fragmentation. Behind the appearance of separation is one unified field of wholeness. Here the seer and the scenery are one." -Deepak Chopra -.*

Chapter Six

> "When we take one step toward God, he takes seven steps
> toward us."
> -- Hindu Proverb-

The Seven Doorways for Transformation

We moved into the group room.

What Keeps Us Stuck?

"What is the rationale behind Souldrama and how did you arrive at the ideas to develop this?"

"This brings to mind the question I asked when I began to develop this program, "What keeps people stuck?""

Milton Erickson (1982) believed that people who are traumatized get stuck in one way of thinking about the world, themselves, and their difficulties. He refers to the fact that it is that "stuckness" that imprisons us, because it knocks us out of connection with our bodies and emotions. It is then that we feel as if we have lost the spirit from our lives. R. D. Laing (1960) talked about the healing process one that brings about facing that shadow parts of ourselves. He said *"When patients are ready, healing dialogues can lead them through the confrontations with death, symbolic death, threatened death, near death, intentional evil, or capricious destructiveness to accept what is given and what is taken away"* (as cited in Schwartz, 2000, p. 448). He said that is what will help a person to feel real and alive, to feel connected. What better way to do this, I thought, than through action methods and psychodrama.

I began to think about the stages in the development of consciousness. There have been many formulations of stages in the development of consciousness that people pass through. These states can be seen as constantly shifting energetic levels of consciousnesses. Each stage of development charts the emergence of a specific developmental potential through a sequence of stages of growth, sometimes called the transcendent formation (van Kaam, 1994). Each stage also steps significantly beyond its predecessors, while including them in an expanded experience of self. One could use the concept of *infrastructure* in the process of consciousness transformation (Blatner, 2004); because it conveys this hierarchical, transcendence, and inclusion aspect, and also reminds us that personal transformation occurs within a social system."

Stages of Development

"Did I miss something in my development? I feel like I missed the beginning of a movie!"

"I was expecting this question. There are developmental lines that occur when we are a child. These were proposed by Anna Freud (1965). The two primary lines of development that are especially important to our health or dysfunction occur during the very early attachment bonding process and the separation-individuation process. Using developmental lines to chart the emergence of developmental potential through a sequence of stages of growth, she stated that pathology can often result from a failure in normal human development in one or more areas. For example, there is a separate line of development consistent with a sense of self (Kohut, 1971), for affect (Brown, 1985), and for the defenses (Vaillant, 1977).

These stage are in mentioned in Maslow's (1943, 1954, 1968, 1971) Hierarchy of Needs. The stages are set out in a hierarchical sequence (the first four were identified in work published in 1943 and 1954; the remaining levels were identified in work published in 1968 and 1971):

(1) Physiological: hunger, thirst, bodily comforts, etc.

(2) Safety/security: out of danger

(3) Belongingness and Love: affiliate with others, be accepted

(4) Esteem: to achieve, be competent, gain approval and recognition

(5) Cognitive: to know, to understand, and explore

(6) Aesthetic: symmetry, order, and beauty

(7) Self-actualization: to find self-fulfillment and realize one's potential

(8) Transcendence: to help others find self-fulfillment and realize their potential

Ken Wilber (2000) believes that there are roughly two dozen developmental lines: "morals, affects, self-identity, psychosexuality, cognition, ideas of the good, role taking, socio-emotional capacity, creativity, altruism, several lines that can be called 'spiritual'(care, openness, concern, religious faith, meditative stages), joy, communicative competence, modes of space and time, death seizure, needs, worldviews, logico-mathematical competence, kinesthetic skills, gender identity, and empathy" (p. 28). He writes about a process of psychospiritual development that we are all going through both as individuals and as members of a historically located culture. There are three broad sections, the prepersonal, the personal, and the transpersonal. As related to the model of Souldrama, I relate these sections to the three levels of our intelligences, the rational, emotional, and the spiritual. Each of these stages, both in Wilbur's and Souldrama are sequential and depend upon the development and completion of the previous stage and in each of these stages we have to revise our notions of who we are or what kind of self we were."

Knock, Knock - Open the Door

"What do the doorways do?"

"The doorways in Souldrama offer symbolic rites of passage and present a challenge for the group to enter transpersonal experience. Let's look at the chart.

Souldrama®: Seven Doors to Spiritual Transformation

One	Two	Three	Four	Five	Six	Seven
			Doorways			
Faith	Truth	Compassion	Love	Humility	Gratitude	Inspiration
Rational IQ		**Emotional IQ**		**Spiritual IQ**		$\frac{IQ}{+}$ $\frac{EQ}{+}$ SQ
What I Think		What I Feel		What I Am		Equals
						UQ Universal Intelligence
Gifts from the Light Messengers Needed to Open the Doors						
Trust	Clarity	Forgiveness	Unconditional Self Love	Empowerment	Self Worth	Transformation

"Wow, in the land of Ego, all our charts are in black and white! These are in color. Can you explain these?"

"Yes, life is very colorful. Let me tell you some more about this chart, moving from the left to the right. Within the process of Souldrama® (Miller, 2008), there are seven sequential pre-determined stages that are used to represent different levels of trust and healing within our journey. Each doorway steps significantly beyond its predecessors, while including them in an expanded experience of self, and as with other developmental lines, this "process of development toward the optimal expression of humanity" proceeds in sequential stages, each one building on and incorporating the earlier stages. In this way, no stage can be skipped and the sequential order of the emerging stages is a relatively fixed aspect of the human experience. Development proceeds by moving beyond the limits of both our personal experience and our experience in a group (Wilber, 2000)."

"Can you say more?"

"Imagine your journey you are about to take to be comprised of seven sequential rooms. Each doorway has a different key to enter and each room is a different color. When you open the doorway to each room you will enter and sense the energy and vibrations and that surround you. Each room has a lesson for you to learn, a challenge to complete, and a gift to receive before you may go on to the next doorway and into the next room. The first two doorways are the most difficult to enter. When you have completed the challenge and received the gift within each doorway, you may leave the peaceful presence of that room in which you learned what you were supposed to and you continue to go on to the next room. You may not even want to leave the room you are in because you are experiencing a new peace. If you stay there, you will have learned all that was necessary. If you choose to enter the next door, you will open up another level of understanding and transformation. Upon the journey, each room will become more beautiful and the silence more intense. Your body will become lighter and less restricted. Each lesson will become clearer, and with each lesson, you will become more present. Each time we enter a new doorway, we can allow the peace and love to enter more easily."

Breaking Down Walls and Opening Doors

"So the first door is where the ego is the fattest or hardest to reduce?"

"Let's look at the chart moving from left to right Miller (2008). Briefly, each door offers a challenge and a gift at the completion of its challenge. Later as we go through these doors, I will talk more about them. For instance, the first two doors comprise our Rational Intelligence and represent the ego or the left brain. The first Door is the door of faith and the gift upon its completion is trust. In order to gain trust, we must be able to surrender (your favorite word, Iye), and give up control to something higher than ourselves. The second door is that of truth, the gift is clarity of your soul's mission. This is where we learn to release the old roles we have played since childhood and embrace our dark side."

"That's scary!"

"It is very natural to be frightened Iye. Remember when we talked about the ego not wanting to give up control? During the first stages of Souldrama, doors one and two, which include our rational intelligence, there is more resistance for when we begin a spiritual journey of any sort, there is more resistance to change from the ego and we stay preoccupied with individual thoughts, images, memories, sensations. Any time we begin a diet or new food plan or any new lifestyle it is difficult to begin as the first few days are the hardest to begin to put new patterns of healthy eating into our lifestyle. Dwelling on the rational content is a definite temptation in early stages of a spiritual journey when something new is introduced that will challenge your old beliefs. This is often the first time you are introduced to the strange, mysterious and exciting world of your inner experience (Engler, 1984). Chögyam Trungpa (2005) says it well. "Since the whole structure of ego is so well fortified against attack, an external invasion is not going to destroy the ego at all. In fact, it is going to reinforce the whole structure because the ego is being given more material with which to work" (p. 47)."

"So this workshop will help me to change? Can you tell me more about the purpose of the doors? They seem fascinating."

"Whitfield (1993) talks about the authentic self "going into hiding" deep within the unconscious part of one's mind. This leaves the false self to try to run the person's life. This process of the real self going into hiding creates even more conflict, dissociation (separation), and isolation of the components of our inner life, which ordinarily should be integrated (Whitfield, 1995). He identifies those components of our inner life to be: beliefs, thoughts, feelings, decisions, choices, experiences, our wants and needs, intuitions, and unconscious experiences, such as fantasies, dreams, and repetition compulsions, as well as our memories. If we can help someone gradually risk safely crossing the doorways, we can help them give up their self-righteous roles that sabotage them and we can help them become aware of their needs and wants, acknowledge them openly, ask for them to be met, and allow someone to do so.

The structure or passage through the doorways offer a ritual or rite of passage that enables one to cross the threshold between the seven doorways of spiritual growth with a conscious awareness of what has been left behind in your spiritual journey and what lies ahead. The separation of the doors by actual physical doorways concretize this feeling in enabling the participant to actually see and feel the passage of one doorway to another and to see their growth. They offer special windows of opportunity to transcend to the next level of growth."

"I don't like the feeling of stepping through a doorway…it seems spooky".

"Iye, remember the old role you played with your father. You thought you needed to have more information and answers to be loved. This is what is coming up here, you are afraid to move forward without all the information and answers. The role you played with your mother of distancing is coming up also as you are afraid to move toward intimacy. This is a time you do not have to" know it all" but if you take the risk to move forward, this will help you to let go and trust someone else to help you. In the transitional space between ego and spiritual intelligence is where we need to unlearn what we have learned- the lessons that were so hard-won in childhood where you learned to separate and not connect to others."

"I hope so."

"The doorways of Souldrama can help bring to consciousness the habitual choices and patterns we make based on old outdated beliefs and roles without becoming engrossed in them. By bringing these choices and patterns to consciousness, we also then have the opportunity to break through our old automated patterns and responses and open that moment to new and spontaneous choices. We learn, within a group situation, how to train to play "new roles" and become conscious, constructing our sense of self anew from moment to moment. When we practice new role behavior and become aware of the old roles we play, we can become free of the preoccupation with the content of our psychic life, free to make spontaneous choices moment to moment, and speak authentically. If we can become conscious of our whole personality, the self, we can become great spiritual leaders by becoming aware of our higher purposes and potential capabilities.

Jack Engler (1984) talks about the connection between Western psychotherapy and Buddhist practices as paths of self-development. He writes, "While ego psychologists might think the meditative goal of non-attachment and disidentification from all self-representations a bit odd if not impossible, they do understand the principle that all psychological growth comes about by being able to renounce outworn, infantile ties to objects and to give up or modify self-representations that have become restrictive, maladaptive or outgrown (p.26). This includes the roles we play."

New Responses to Old Roles

"Deepak Chopra (2000) talks about different levels of fulfillment and the seven responses of the human brain as avenues to attain some aspect of God. These seven responses apply to the doors of Souldrama. Door One: Faith (Flight or Fight Response); Door Two: Clarity (Reactive Response); Door Three: Compassion: (Restful Awareness Response); Door Four: Love (Intuitive Response); Door Five; Humility: (Creative Response); Door Six; Gratitude (Visionary Response) Door Seven: Inspiration (Sacred Response). To go further, the flight or fight comes from the choice of fear, reactive response comes from the choice of power to compete and achieve, restful awareness response comes from choice for inner reflection, intuitive response comes from the choice to gain insight, creative response comes from the choice to create and discover newness, the visionary response comes from a choice to act with deference and the sacred response comes from the choice to want to heal others and yourself and from a choice to appreciate the infinite scope of possibilities."

"This sounds wonderful! Do the three levels of intelligence correspond to the left and right brain?"

"These three major levels of intelligence, the rational corresponds to the left brain (what I think), the emotional (what I feel) to the gap in-between both sides and the spiritual (what I am) to the right brain. The Buddhists talk about three "thirsts" in life that correspond to the rational, emotional, and spiritual intelligences to free you from the false internalized roles within; the thirst for pleasure, the thirst for existence, and the thirst for non-existence. These by chance, correspond to the three levels of intelligence on the chart. What we want to do is to balance all three intelligences."

"So what you are saying is that Souldrama offers one method to consciously transform to a higher level of self, or a self beyond a self while connecting the left and right brain?"

"Yes!"

The Space In Between the Doors

"I can see that the colors fade from one doorway to the next-how come they fade into each other?"

"The spaces in between the doorways can serve as gateways through which we can enter transpersonal experience, cross thresholds of consciousness, and offer a transitional space for stepping from where you are now into a new higher level of functioning. Each time we grow and change, we need to have space in which to integrate our work. Winnicott (1965a) called this a transitional space. In other words, Souldrama offers a safe holding environment so that group members can move from one doorway to another, from childhood ego dependence into adult ego independence and eventually to ego transcendence.

Waldron (1998) indicates that there are three general phases of integration of transcendent experience during the transitional time. The first is coming into balance with the initial impact of the experience. Transitional space is often chaotic and balance is most easily found when a solid infrastructure of support exists, both intra psychically and socially. This is provided by the group. The second phase integrates the experience and its meaning into a person's life as he /she moves toward improved psychological health and spiritual growth. This is where you may have "life turning-points, that is, watersheds leading to underlying long-term internal change, with a sense of before and after which is of high significance" (Ahern, 1990, p.41), and may reorganize your life around the meaning of your inspirational experience. The third phase of integration is creatively expressing the meaning in the world, in some form of action that would directly or indirectly be helpful to others. Integrating the experience and reorganizing your life usually involves contributing to society."

"How does an individual develop that security to explore? I am terrified!"

"Such security normally develops early in life when, ideally, the child balances attachment (freedom from fear of abandonment) with detachment (freedom from fear of engulfment), resulting in liberation from the control of either (the freedom to explore the external and internal worlds), (Lowe, 2000). When a child does not get that security, the group becomes the reconstructive family of origin giving you what you did not get in your family."

"Oh, you mean we need to crawl before we can walk? So when we are children and we grow and develop there is a transitional space in between stages of development as well?"

"Yes, for it is in the times in between the developmental stages that offer the healthy transitional space to develop socially and psychologically. It is important that we have childhoods for when we are children we learn to have the ability to play with spontaneity, to live both in fantasy and reality, the ability to be alone and to be intimate with others.

Keep reminding yourself that before a time of change there may be chaos. Transitional space is the personal space between security, which is secure attachment to the group and freedom for yourself in which to trust yourself as you grow and know that you can stand on your own. This time can be very empowering or frightening, depending on how you choose to see it. In each doorway the ego becomes secure enough so that it will risk leaving order and predictability to move into the chaos of unpredictability of the next doorway of transformation. After you complete the first doorway, you will be in a transitional space until you go through the next sequential doorway. During these times, part of you will be surrendering your old roles and belief systems. The other part will be open to consciousness during which you will you have moments perhaps including meditation, dreams, trance states, shamanic states, sacred, or mystical moments. So you may finish one Souldrama workshop Iye and then be left working with a special light messenger after you leave the workshop."

The Light Messengers

"You said this word before -a what? Light Messenger-what is that? Is this some type of religious cult? Now you are freaking me out a bit."

"The rites of the passage through the doorways were designed to build in anchors or Light Messengers to remind the participant to stay conscious and mindful during times of transition. Each doorway has a

Light Messenger©. Each Light Messenger offers a gift, a color and a symbol to give us an anchor to act as the transitional object to help us navigate in between the doorways.

Times of transition are challenging for us to maintain the new healthy patterns we have learned; therefore, it is good to have anchors to call upon in these times of need, confusion and chaos. An anchor is any stimulus that evokes a consistent emotional response pattern from a person. The anchor is always connected to one's integrity, morals, values, and priorities, or one's authentic self. Symbols and colors are also a way to remind ourselves of our true purpose when we become distracted. Symbols have been around for ages. Plato in the Symposium cites Eros as a mighty daimon, halfway between God and man. Eros, always present in the unconscious background of the psyche, animates the inner world and keeps the channels open between the ego and the unconscious (the collective psyche); in a potential space Jung called the 'transcendent function' (as cited in Kalsched, 2003). Your light messenger is your damion, a spirit, an invisible assistant, that accompanies you throughout your journey, even after you leave the workshop. "Our daimons are catalysts we can use to get in touch with our inner genius. They act as a bridge between the four functions (thinking, intuition, feeling, sensate) and the transcendent function. This is a way "we are able to elevate the conscious mind beyond the boundaries of ego" (Cavalli, 2002, p. 57). We use seven light messengers as the Damions.

In the Buddhist psychology of spiritual development, there are six "worlds" or realms. Each realm has a known anchor to assist the person to awaken, thereby escaping his imaginary prison, and fulfilling the opportunity presented in that realm. Giving you an anchor from the light messenger is similar to classical conditioning where you can associate an internal response."

"When I was a child, I had a blanket for security when I was growing up-I never wanted to give it up. Was this an anchor or transitional object for me?"

"Yes. Sometimes it is a stuffed animal or an imaginary friend. This object is a first step in the child's separation from mother, a substitute for the mother's care that provides a feeling of safety for a child. The transitional object allows the child to feel safe and supported within which to move from a purely personal experience to one in which there is a clear distinction between "me" and "other." The transitional object enjoys a special in-between status, neither "me" nor "other," but somehow both.

Let's look at the first doorway of Faith. For example the symbol for the first messenger is the triangle and the gift it offers is trust. The purpose of this doorway is to access our faith and to surrender to something higher than ourselves."

"Hey, this is the symbol for Alcoholics Anonymous. So after I go through the first doorway, Faith, each time I see the symbol of the triangle, I will be reminded to have faith and to trust what is happening."

"Now you are getting it. The passions and energies of human beings can be aroused by symbols. Fischer and Landon (1972) showed that the introduction of a highly significant, arousal-inducing symbol can further increase the already existing level of arousal. Fischer (1975-1976) concludes, "State-bound memories, then, may be 'flashbacks' either on an individual or species level and they refer to that Platonic knowledge, 'which is already there,' the human program laid down in not more than a dozen or so (archetypal) great stories, pictures, statues, and songs which are re-created, written, composed, sculpted and sung by each generation." (p. 364).

"It is difficult for me to ask for help. Sometimes, the only time I feel I can be myself is when I am alone."

"Of course, many of us feel that way for this is when you can finally get role relief. Remember, when we were talking about our development? Winnicott (1957) said, it is important for the personality to be able to rest between structures of development, to stop doing, and just be in the state of nothingness where one takes time off from self. It is important to have time between choices, time simply to be. What a relief not to have to be this or that, not to have to force oneself into a particular role or have to "shape up" (Eigen, 1992, p. 272). This transitional time is needed before we take the next step of transformation. This is where you are open to receive, to relax boundaries, and to allow the past and future to fade away. As boundaries diminish, the sense of self becomes less distinct and less contained; the ego becomes more aligned with the soul."

"So sometimes I really want to change and other times I think I am fine! What is this about?"

"The ego's connection with the soul varies through the day perhaps like our moods. It is normal to have transitions between states of growth and it is then that we can remember the symbol of the light messengers and we can also use things such as rituals, prayer and meditation, music, etc to boost the sense of connection between the ego and the soul. During transitional states, we begin to identify less with the ego and as we go through the doorways we begin to open to unity, synchronicity, transcendence of space and time, the sense of sacredness, bliss, and impermanence."

"In other words the ego becomes thinner?"

"Yes. Or another word is disintegrated."

"Well. Now we have talked and you have explained things, I think I really think I am ready to go to the door of unconditional love. I can skip doors one, two and three as I am ready for love."

"Patience, Iye."

"So what happens if I skip doorways?"

"One of the great dangers of transformational work is that the ego attempts to sidestep deep psychological work by leaping into the world of spiritual intelligence too soon. This is because the ego always thinks that it is much more advanced than it actually is. The ego brings forth resistance and in each stage, more of the ego is aligned with the soul. When we begin a healing journey, either in therapy or on a spiritual path, we need time and space so that we can do integrative work. The doorways provide the transitional space which is a personal space between security (secure attachment) and autonomy (freedom to explore).

If you skip over the sequence of the doorways, you will miss those opportunities to grow during this transitional time between doorways. We need to go through the doorways one at a time. Each doorway moves us through the resistance of the ego creating a strong net of safety in which we can let go and trust. Imagine being on a trapeze bar swinging over to reach the next bar. In between the two bars you have to let go –the space between the bars is the transitional space for transformation, for it is the space between the notes that makes the music!"

"This makes sense because if I keep on playing the same note over and over life, it would be boring and there would be no music, just the same old tune. The music is made when we move from one note to another."

"Well done, Iye. So it is with life and playing the same old roles over and over. It is in the risking change and let go of old roles and moving on to new ones that we can hear more music. Again imagine using the analogy of the trapeze, in between the trapeze bars, one must stay very present. If we try to hurry the process up and become impatient by wanting to move on the next bar, or moving through to the next level of growth that we think we need, we will miss the next bar and fall. You may be frightened to grab the next bar, by fear of success, fear of failure, shame and unworthiness, or by unwillingness to grieve losses or accept the mission of transcendence. Likewise, if we skip doorways, unresolved grief, grudges, resentments, unfulfilled promises, or unexpressed anger will appear later. When we are that space of nothingness, in between the bars, we have the opportunity to learn to be present to hear and see all those opportunities offered to us to change. If we identify with the ego, we will have many anxieties, including fear of life and fear of death. When we can dissolve this identification, our fears will dissolve."

"Then I can ask, "Where did my ego go?" We both laughed.

> *"No problem can be solved on the same level at which you meet it."*
>
> - Einstein-

Chapter Seven

Intuit and Do It!

Iye: *"Tell me about intuition."*

"Let's call intuition our still small voice within."

"Like when I knew my last date was not going to show up?"

"Yes, perhaps that is how come it is called a "blind date." Maybe next time you have a date you will be wide awake!" We laughed.

"We all have access to the power of intuition though we rarely develop its potential. Our intuition is part of our unconscious intelligence and it complements rational thinking and decision making. Antonio Damasio (1994), a neurologist who has studied the links between cognitive and emotional intelligence, believes that intuition is the glue that holds together our conscious intellect and our intelligent action."

"Is this what we mean by a gut feeling?"

"You may experience your intuition as a gut feeling, or as an inner sense of what is right or wrong for you. Sometimes, your intuition manifests itself as a hunch or an inspiration or a flash of insight. Your intuition leads you to new ideas, concepts, and breakthroughs. Sometimes, an intuitive flash will enable you to see a problem from a new perspective and allow you to solve it on a completely different level. It has been said that men and women start to become great when they begin to listen to their inner voice, or their intuition. Intuition is so powerful that it has been studied and written about for thousands of years by some of the greatest men and women in history. When you begin to use it regularly, there is almost nothing that you cannot accomplish.

As Einstein said "No problem can be solved on the same level at which you meet it." This means that the more you do what you're doing, the more you'll get of what you've got, so trying to solve your current problem at your current level is often useless. You can unlock your intuition by using your imagination to think about your problem in a totally different way.

Men and women who have a highly developed imagination have often reached the point where they completely trust their intuition — their inner voice — to guide them in every situation. The never speak or act until they feel an inner urging to do so. They know that their intuition will always bring them exactly the right answer at exactly the right time. The most successful individuals throughout history have been those who have deliberately trained themselves to tap into their creative imagination on a regular basis using their intuition.

Your intuition leads to a form of intelligence that is accessed by your subconscious mind, which is controlled by the thoughts you think and the beliefs you hold in your conscious mind. The more often you affirm and visualize your desired goals in your conscious mind, the more readily they are picked up by your subconscious mind, and the more rapidly your intuition or creative imagination is triggered. Successful, effective, and happy people are those who rely on their own intuitive senses and their inner guidance — and they seldom make mistakes."

"Will the woman of my dreams have more intuition than me? I have heard the term woman's intuition."

"Women's intuition is more respected than men's because they trust it more. Women are generally very respectful of their intuitive feelings and they generally refuse to go against them. The truth is that men and women have intuitions that are equally accurate. They seem to come up with the same intuitive answers to complex problems and questions. Women listen to their intuition more, while men tend to brush it aside. When a woman says, "This situation doesn't feel right," she trusts this feeling as a valid and important assessment of whether the situation is right or wrong. Men will often brush aside their intuitive leanings in favor of a short-term conscious solution to meet a short term goal, only to pay the price later."

"This sounds like my last marriage. I told myself not to get involved with her but then I pretended that she was really not that way, and boy did I pay the price! Sex is a great short term goal! How do I get more intuition?"

"Again, we do not *get* this, as we all have it. This is what we need to access when we access our SQ. When we close our minds with our ego, we shut off hearing the voice of intuition. When we keep our minds open, we can begin to imagine all sorts of new possibilities! We need to stop cluttering up our heads with noise. We cannot hear the wise voice of our intuition if we are always thinking and talking and being distracted by outer events. Intuition can flourish, given space and time for reflection. If you are often under stress, you will find it difficult to be intuitive even though we all have this potential. To develop your intuition, it will help to expand your ability for "relaxed attention." Have you had the experience that the harder you try to achieve a task, the more difficult it becomes? There is a difficult way that involves worry, increasing effort, and frustration at your delay in making a decision. The easy way is to ease off, take a break, and trust that your intuition will help you find a new direction."

Be Still

"What do I need to do to stimulate my intuition?"

"Perhaps the best method for stimulating your intuition is to practice solitude on a regular basis. It is important to take time daily to experience physical stillness and to direct our attention inside, where we can begin to find the peace, love, will and wisdom that exist as our essence. We cannot hear the wise voice of intuition if we are always thinking, talking, and being distracted by outer events. Try and practice daily stillness, direct your attention inside and you will begin to find the peace and wisdom that is there.

Throughout the ages, spiritual leaders practiced solitude regularly in their work and life. They took time to be alone with themselves. They went off and sat quietly prior to any situation of importance. Most of the great leaders of today continue to use solitude as an essential tool in developing the creative insights and intuitions that often have the power to change lives. All the great writers, composers, artists, and scientists have developed the habit of listening to their intuition. You have access to the same intuitive powers as the smartest men and women who ever lived."

"So if I sit and try to get an answer, I will?"

"Again, Iye, this is not about trying to get something from outside of yourself but about *being* something. If you have a question that needs resolving, try to sit in solitude. Solitude requires no "doing". It simply requires a state of relaxed awareness in which you open your mind to your greater intelligence. At the right moment, exactly the right answer you need will come to you in exactly the right form."

"I don't have the time for this!"

"We cannot afford not to practice solitude on a regular basis. Most people have never practiced solitude because they believe that they have no time for it. However, one good idea that comes to you in the silence of solitude can save you a year of hard work. When you are deeply involved in what you are doing, perhaps for you of taking photographs and absorbed in that activity, you experience a loss of self-consciousness, which may be considered self-transcendence. This is a state of tapping into the mystical experience (non-ego experience) of oneness, of radical connectedness. Csikszentmihalyi (1993) describes such a transcending person as one who harmoniously combines opposite tendencies: "he or she is original yet systematic, independent yet responsible, bold yet disciplined, intuitive yet rational" (p. 238)."

"Well that seems worth it. You mean it is that easy to access the unconscious?"

"Actually, your own true experiences seem to find expression, often through unconscious means such as when you dream. While the unconscious may be out of awareness, it directly influences behavior. Corsini (2000) said dreams, slips of the tongue, forgetting, delusions, and projections are a few of the many common ways that the unconscious finds expression. On some level the soul tries to express itself through unconscious means.

Jung believed that the need to reconnect to the Self is instinctual; therefore, the effort to do so occurs either consciously or unconsciously (as cited in Jacobi, 1965). When we remain in old roles and patterns of behavior, we don't know what to do with certain new information or learning. Even though the unconscious may be out of awareness, it directly influences behavior for eventually this repressed information interferes with functioning, and we become mentally exhausted by the great amount of energy required to maintain the illusion of the self. This imbalance is considered to be at the core of neurotic behaviors (Corsini, 2000). Much of our own knowledge comes to us from our previous experience of the world. Each time we encounter a new and difficult situation we need to have knowledge of ourselves as much as any facts. In a world filled with noise we need to quiet our minds to hear the voice of God."

"What else access the unconscious?"

"There are many passive states of healing that help you to access the unconscious that require you to be open and to be receptive: free association, psychodrama, dream work, hypnotic age regression, breath work, and shamanic work. Dr. William Roll (1968) believed that consciousness may survive death. He called this thetaconsciousness. According to Roll, thetaconsciousness extends beyond the body and shows itself in out-of-body experiences, transpersonal and mystical states, deathlike or near-death states, and consciousness after physical death. We may approach this same theta state in meditation as well. Singh (1998)"

"So we extend beyond ourselves? This is really freaking me out now. What good does meditation do?"

"If we want to begin to hear the still small voice within we can begin to choose to consciously meditate as a way to become more aware of whom we truly are. Meditation helps us to break through old roles and masks that we have seen as our identity, break through our defenses and connect with the parts of ourselves that feel unloved. Meditation calms our minds and makes it easier for us to pay attention to the reality around and within us. It opens us up to our higher selves as it also teaches us to be present."

"I often have day dreams and I cannot explain them because they are not logical and made no sense. Sometimes I wake up with the best ideas!"

"We often think over their problems just before going to sleep and get a solution in our dreams or immediately upon awakening. This is because our minds were so active on the intellectual plane that we could not make contact with the silent inner plane where ideas work. Try to remember to keep a piece of paper by your bed to write those dreams down.

Emotional and spiritual intelligence are connected to the unfolding of self through developing specific skills. The continued practice of dream work leads to the development of the skills of metaphoric and imagistic thinking, appreciation of dream nuances, understanding of the body-mind boundaries, intentional dreaming, openness to guidance, and empathy (Deslauriers, 2000). When the conscious mind is stilled and one makes contact with the super consciousness, it begins to show us how our affairs will work out or how we can help to bring about the desired outcomes."

"It sounds like it is worth giving it a try."

"You can overcome any obstacle, solve any problem, or achieve any goal by tapping into the incredible powers of your mind and by trusting your intuition. Once you begin to develop and use your intuition, you will become more alert, more aware, smarter, and more effective in everything that you do. I hope that this process will help you go forth and learn to trust your intuition."

"So let's intuit and do it!"

> *I have discovered that all human evil comes from this;*
> *man's being unable to sit still in a room.*
>
> *-Blaise Pascal-*

Chapter Eight

> *"We need people in our lives with whom we can be as open as possible. To have real conversation with people may seem like such a simple, obvious suggestion, but it involves courage and risk."*
>
> *-Thomas Moore-*

The Power of a Group

I Can Do This Alone

"I am a very private person. I don't need to share all my problems with other people and least of all I do not need to sit and hear others talk about theirs. Sometimes I think my problems are not bad at all when I hear theirs".

I knew that it was going to a real challenge to convince Iye of the power of a group.

"Remember where you live. In the state of Ego you think with the left brain. You told me how alone you feel. If we begin to read the books alone, do the work alone and to compare ourselves to others, then we are separating ourselves from our soul and feeding the ego. The need for belonging is a universal trait. The fellowship of a group today is important to remove the "I" from the ego because today in our Western world, we seem to think that our recognition comes from competition; from acquiring and hoarding more material possessions and from excelling in this world. Most miracles happen through other people. To gather the greatest benefits from intuition, we need to take action and allow ourselves to be in front of more opportunities and people. It is important to let go of any blocks or attachments and to create both mental space and physical space. People are the hands of God, so when we join with others who are trying to grow spiritually, we have a different set of values; compassion, giving, generosity of the heart, service, truth, time and support. Joining a group is a very important and dynamic process for spiritual growth. There is no more

"I", but a sense of "we". It is in a group that we begin to see ourselves in relationship to others and we begin to connect again.

What seems to hold religions together more than anything is the sense of community and relationships; the fact that we are a large family rather than a large belief system. There is a common interest and we know that we are linked to something more important than the ego and personal opinions. We need to begin to connect to other people who are on a conscious spiritual path. The fellowship of like-minded people attracts grace for when we are around people who are committed to spiritual awakening; we begin to resonate at the same energy level."

"Maybe that is what I am afraid of. I do want to stop isolating but I have no idea how others see me."

How Do You See Me?

"It is in a group that we see ourselves in relationship to others. Now let's talk about group consciousness. Zerka Moreno (1965), wife of the father of group therapy, J L Moreno, said we were born in a group, learned our roles in a group and we can be healed in a group. In a group there is a sense of Holism where we can see larger patterns, relationships, and connections."

"It makes sense that since we developed our roles in a group that is the place to transform them!"

"The dramatic nature of psychodrama builds group cohesion and support. Group members begin to hold one another responsible for their behavior. Meanwhile participants also begin to recognize their own responsibility for change. By taking responsibility, individuals become empowered -- a critical step in personal transformation. The group focuses on involvement, belonging and aspects of relationships. Being in a group brings up concerns about ethics, conscience and awareness of one another. There is a feeling of justice because of the love of someone else or an ideal. This aspect of justice of conscience is the basis of love for one another and makes us human with the ability to reflect, create, and form boundaries. Our families of origin were not necessarily a chosen group. The idea of good group cohesion comes from giving people choices (Z.Moreno, 2000). When we make poor choices, we need therapy or we learn what we need to for our soul to grow. Sociometry, the measurement of human relations, deals with human relationships in terms of role interaction with significant others on the private level, on the professional level, and on the community level. One of Moreno's (1945) ideals was that many people are forced into relationships that are not mutually productive and we would do far better if we allowed people to have their choices even if it meant that choices must be changed. When choices change, it is because our role interactions change and society should be flexible enough to allow for that. One of the reasons one enters therapy is because of the poor choices they have made in life.

Psychodrama is the action methodology for the science of action. Often it is described as a laboratory for learning how to love, where the patient's inner world can match the outer world. It is a place where love and acceptance of the worst aspects of ourselves is found, where we can experience our own humanity and learn how to transcend the past to reach for a more promising future.

Zerka Moreno (1965) has described the group as the "double for life", saying that group consciousness reflects the spiritual and moral ideals of society and is the foundation of our society's rules and laws. In a group, we expose our darker sides and experience the cathartic effect of being re-admitted to the group. J.L. Moreno believed that there is no authority than what comes from the entire group itself; each person of the group is the therapeutic agent of the other."

"I am so ashamed of and feel so guilty about some of my past actions."

"You are not alone with these feelings either. Yalom (1975) observed that individual group members find encouragement and hope by seeing others in the group in varying stages of transformation! Yalom (1975) found that many individuals believe that their problems are unique when they feel alone, afraid, and shameful."

"So I am not alone? I thought my problems were special."

"Existential factors come into play via the powerful experience of psychodrama. Group members gain an awareness of the universal nature of pain, death, aloneness, and individual responsibility (Yalom, 1975). These struggles become a shared experience and thereby reduce the associated shame and fear so often felt. It is a commonly held belief that one's own experience is the ultimate teacher. One aspect of this wisdom is the notion that we learn about ourselves by being in relationships with others (Yalom, 1975). The interpersonal focus of the psychodrama group allows for dynamic person-to-person interaction. In the psychodrama group, this interaction promotes corrective emotional experiences as members begin to express long-held emotions and begin to clarify interpersonal boundaries and limits. The group offers a supportive, safe place to begin this process. As group members become more conscious regarding their own patterns of interpersonal relating, a clarity emerges which can only be gained by an intensive group interaction such as using a method like psychodrama. One way group members learn new behaviors is by picking up on and trying out healthy behaviors displayed by others in the group. Albert Bandura (1977) found modeling to be an important facet in learning. Moreover, Bandura (1977) emphasized that role playing new behaviors can deepen the learning process. Psychodrama provides an opportunity to try out these behaviors.

The Energy of a Group

Within the environment of a supportive group, members can share feelings with others and realize their experiences are universal to all humans. Group members are fully accepted in spite of their weaknesses, feelings of shame, and isolation subside. Transformational group methods like psychodrama facilitate the revelation that others have similar problems thereby reducing isolation and alienation (Moreno, 1971)."

"*I am beginning to feel better. How did group psychotherapy start. I do go to AA, is that like it?*"

"As one of the first to develop the group therapy format, Moreno (1971) spent most of his career refining different forms of group counseling, including psychodrama (as cited in Johnson, 1999) to promote dynamic group interaction. Alcoholics Anonymous is a support group not a therapy group. The first Twelve Step group began when Moreno started to work with prostitutes from the streets of Vienna. Already condemned as sinners who were beyond help, he sought to restore some sense of hope and empowerment. To this end, he had them meet in groups of ten, three times a week. They began to share the details of their lives such as trouble with difficult "clients" or worries over their children. Eventually, as trust grew, emotion was more freely expressed as the deeper truths of their lives began to spill forward. Through identification with each other and opening up, sharing their stories and taking in the support of a non-judgmental group, they began to heal and their lives started to improve. This represented the earliest attempts to treat people in groups; up until this date clients had only been treated one on one. Thus, J.L. Moreno is considered to be the father of group therapy."

"Wow, and I was feeling ashamed-imagine how those prostitutes felt!"

"A large and important part of our spiritual journey is the power and the fellowship of the group. Gathering with other spiritual seekers creates a receptivity that we can all tap into. As we come together and work together to awaken our higher purpose, we bring the focus of our attention onto God, truth, beauty, love, and service and delve deeper into that awareness. The group energy amplifies the work. We are not passive vessels for God's will. To realize our highest potential, we must co-create with the divine and that means other people as well.

Tomorrow we begin the workshop so perhaps we should get a good night's rest. Thank you for letting me explain the purpose of the workshop to you and thank you for your research as well. I am getting very tired."

Iye nodded. *"Good night!"*

Chapter Nine

> *"It often seems easier not to move on; even the muck and mire in which we're stuck seems less fearful and less challenging than the unknown path ahead. Some people use faith as a reason to remain stuck. They often say, "I have faith, so I'm waiting." But faith is not complacent; faith is action. You don't have faith and wait. When you have faith, you move. Complacency actually shows lack of faith. When it's time to move in a new direction in order to progress, the right people will come to us."*
>
> *-Betty Eadie-*

Door One: The Challenge of Faith

The Gift: Trust

The next morning we were ready to begin the Souldrama® workshop.

"Are you ready to begin the workshop, Iye? Or maybe I should call the workshop the challenge of the doors!"

"I am." Iye said tentatively as walked into the group room, looked around and saw seventeen other participants and almost backed out the door.

"Let me remind you that the purpose of this door is to help us give up control and find a safe way to connect with our higher power. We can compare this workshop to a pilgrimage that facilitates saying goodbye to past experiences with grace while courageously facing an unfolding life with intent and purpose. Remember, all therapy is about taking risks to do something different.

I am sure the other participants are feeling a bit scared like you but remember they have come here for much the same reason as you."

"That makes me feel better." Iye said with relief.

"Let's meet the other group members. Welcome everyone. It is a bit chilly in the room so let's warm up.

The goal of the first doorway in Souldrama is to build trust among ourselves as we ask for help to give up control and find a safe way to connect with our higher power. One way to do this is as a group is to warm up to each other. We will be using trust building activities during this process to link commonalities between ourselves, build group cohesion, reduce anxiety, and encourage here-and-now interactions. One of the tools that we will use and that I will talk more about later is sociometry. We are also going to play! (Here the members looked at me strangely.) Warming up is a mixture of action, group dynamics, play, and other techniques that serve to heighten spontaneity gradually throughout the process of our journey this week. Play offers a dimension that allows us to drop our preconceived ideas of this workshop and I am sure many of you have different ideas. (They nodded). Laughter and fun helps us to let go of control.

Let's make a show of confidentiality by joining one hand together in the middle of the room and agree verbally that what was discussed here in this workshop will remain here. Now if you are ready lets meet each other. I am drawing an invisible line down the center for the room. Please stand somewhere on this line. The far end represents the number ten meaning "I am very comfortable in a group" and the near end represents a one meaning "I am not at all comfortable in a group."

Iye stood on the number one, not surprisingly; however, he was not alone. Standing with him were three other group members. The other group members were scattered randomly along the continuum. Mary stood alone on the highest level being an eight.

"Please share with the person nearest to you your fears or comforts of being in a group."(Iye immediately became busy talking to the person next to him.) "Now stand somewhere on the line where you would like to be at the end of the workshop and share with the member next to you what you would like to accomplish. Each member moved up the line. Now please lets each share with the entire group what it may take for you to get there."

Iye moved to a level 5 and shared *"I will really need to learn to trust."*

"I am now putting down some cards face down on the floor. On the opposite side you will find something written. When I say "go" please hold your card face up and find your partner that will be holding the matching card…. such as up-down; plus-minus. Go!"

Iye: *"I have the word, Left". (Not coincidentally) "Where is my opposite? Oh, there you are holding the word Right. You are the woman who was standing at the end of the line Number 8 representing your level of comfort being in a group. Your name is Mary!"*

"When you have found your partner, please sit down and share three things you have in common with each other and then we will introduce your new friend and share with the group what you have found in common."

Iye: *"Mary and I were brought up in the same village in the state of Ego and we each have two children and have been married two times. We both love to read and do photography. She now lives in the land of Soul. I am so surprised. Did you set this up?"*

"No", I assured him. "Often we wonder how we find each other. Faith is about taking action as we just did as a group."

Mary: '*This is my fourth time coming to a Souldrama workshop. The first time, I stood where Iye did but now I find that I am comfortable standing on the level 8, even though no one was standing next to me. I hope this reassures you Iye. Today, I was the only one who had no partner to talk with because I stood on a high number representing my comfort level of being in a group. So even though I was more comfortable, it was lonelier there. I noticed you at least had a group to talk to.*"

"Thank you", said Iye. *"I am so surprised that I found someone so comfortable in a group and with so much in common!"*

"The question for us in this workshop is what needs to be unlearned in order to move forward in our lives? What does the ego need from the soul? What is stopping us from moving forward? The participants nodded their heads. The first thing we need is the ability to relax and trust in a safe environment. That is what you will do for each other over the course of this week.

The purpose of the first Door is to surrender and have faith in a "power higher than ourselves" and trust that there is a, God or a 'Greater Wholeness of Being'. Here, we invoke the process of prayer or meditation."

Let Go and Let God

"How does prayer tie into this process?" asked Iye.

"All the ways of spiritual growth talk about "letting go" or surrendering. When we pray it is a way to let go and let God in. Prayer is about having a shift in perception that there is something greater than ourselves-moving from the awareness of separation to an awareness of our oneness with the presence. There is a sense of full dimensional thinking. It is a matter of faith that by letting go of the mind, you access something greater - call it the mystery of the greater mind or the mystery of nature. By letting go of control, you give control to something that not only transcends the mind but has its own greater laws. It is often a way to remind ourselves often of our spiritual natures. The process of prayer truly can change the quality of our lives by helping us to relax, slow down and lighten up."

"There is a familiar motto, Let Go and Let God. This is in my twelve step program!"

"Sometimes, we become so exhausted that we do let God in. When we pray, we are admitting to the ego that something greater than it exists; therefore, constant contact with our higher power through prayer is a good thing. I suggest prayer as a method to encourage spiritual surrender and facilitate relaxation and trust among ourselves and as a reminder that we are not all powerful. While surrendering, we are also trusting we are connected to a greater whole and higher power. The goal of this doorway is to obtain a high level of trust which is essential for us to commit passionately to our paths without attachment to the outcome (Miller, 2000). Soren Kierkegaard said "The function of prayer is not to influence God, but rather to change the nature of the one who prays."

Here we consider the concepts in the Serenity Prayer (AA, n.d.):
God, grant me the Serenity,
To accept the things I cannot change…
Courage to change the things I can,
And Wisdom to know the difference.

Now, please be seated and introduce yourself briefly to the group sharing what attracted you to this workshop and also what you would like to take home with you from this workshop when you leave."

Colleen: *"I would like to have serenity although I'm not sure I even know what that is."*

"Boyd-Wilson et al. (2004) worked to identify the components of serenity and found these: Faith, Humility, and Gladness. "These qualities are found in people who tend to feel loving and connected meaningfully to the world, who are notably resilient, and who have a profound overall sense of trust. Serene people also tend to take things one day at a time, and have a good sense of how they fit into the scheme of things, neither inflating nor minimizing their role, but actively changing things for the better where they can and accepting situations where they are unable to change them. Serenity in this sense involves enthusiasm for life rather than simply a feeling of calm" (p. 35).

"Serenity is viewed as a learned, positive emotion of inner peace that can be sustained. It is a spiritual concept that decreases perceived stress and improves physical and emotional health. The experience of serenity is related to development of the higher self. There are four levels of serenity that include a safe, wise, beneficent, and universal self" (Roberts & Whall, 1996, p. 359).

"In the twelve steps, they mention surrendering our life and will to God. Surrendering to me implies becoming a victim", said Maria.

"In the process of surrendering, we encounter and are receptive to something that moves us and is in part outside of our control. This means we must be receptive and vulnerable to another. This is different than being passive as being receptive implies being in a state of co-creation with another. In the moment of surrender, a person demonstrates willingness and an openness to be moved by another. This includes the recognition of our own as well as the others needs and desires in order to generate new experiences. This is not the same as victim perpetrator for that implies making another person an object, or losing oneself in the presence of the other which is called codependency.

During surrender one has experience of being totally present and alive which is connected to the discovery of one's identity and sense of self, even ones unity with other living beings. There is no submission or dominance. Surrender is necessary for a true sense of self and aliveness making it safe to risk stating ones desires and needs. True surrender requires mutual receptivity and vulnerability. I hope as the group leader, we can all experience this and have a sense of co creation with each other and know that we are all one.

You seem to be more comfortable with each other. Now please stand on the line again but this time the line will represent how comfortable you are with your own spirituality today." Iye surprisingly stood on a 2.5.

He shared *"Two days ago I would have been on a zero. Since that time we have talked about spirituality and a spiritual journey. Now I am feeling more at ease and excited about moving forward- in fact I already have. I am glad that my partner, Mary is standing on a 9 because perhaps she can help me grow."*

"Take the time now to share about your own spiritual journey with the person next to you. Then we will take a short break."

Iye came over and said, *"This is not so bad, but kind of cool! I am feeling so much better!"*

Play is Universal

After the break, we continued the workshop. "I notice that we are from all different lands and cultures. Many of you speak different languages. No matter what land I am in I always try to remember that the deepest feelings of pain, joy, and love have no words. They are cross-cultural and connect us all. The tools we use here use psychodrama and action methods to help us access our feelings. We all like to play, this is universal."

"What is psychodrama you mentioned that before", asked Bill.

"Psychodrama is essentially an existential encounter between a group of people. By employing a social network to facilitate deep change, J.L.Moreno, founder of psychodrama, group psychotherapy, and sociometry, invited people to live out the Golden Rule, reversing roles and imagining what it may be like to be the other person, promoting empathy, compassion, and self-reflection (Blatner, 2000). As a young man, Moreno would observe children at play in the parks of Vienna. He observed that the children would use role play, to resolve through action, the life issues that were bothering them. As they played out their own role of "baby" for example they might whine, cry, and stomp their feet for attention. They would then "reverse roles" into the "mother" and supply themselves with the attention and understanding or discipline that they may or not wish for. Essentially they would be teaching the other child how to become the corrective mother. As such, the children had the opportunity to "act out" their identification with the role of aggressor in play rather than in real life. This provided the corrective emotional experience. We are here to do that with each other today so let's become like children.

I would like each of you to choose some scarves of different colors and put them on and become your favorite fantasy character from childhood. Now walk around and become that character and introduce yourselves to each other. "(The members become loud and spontaneous.) "Now introduce yourself to the group and staying in the role of your character say how you, as that character, will yourself move forward this week."

Iye stepped out into the middle of the circle *"I am superman and I have courage and strength and vision. I am here to help Iye this week know that he has the courage to change and when he feels frightened to help him along. I want to give him the confidence he needs, and like Clark Kent, have him know he is much more underneath. I want him to know that he does not have to change his identity to be in a relationship, but simply be himself."*

Iye's partner, Mary, was Wonder Woman. She said *"I am here to help fight injustice. I want Mary to know that sometimes things do not seem fair but there is always a lesson in them."*

"You make a good pair! Now, please continue to introduce yourselves to the group as the fantasy character you chose and invite the other members to ask you questions how that fantasy character will help you to grow this week".

Meeting the Messengers of Light

"That was fun. Now, I would like to introduce you to the "Messengers of Light,©" As I put the pictures of the light messengers face up on the floor in a circle stand by the one that attracts you the most. Nothing is written on the front of the pictures. Now when it is your turn, please read the message on the back of the picture you chose out loud to the group."

It was Iye's turn and he became the spokesperson for his group. He read: *"The Messengers of Light: Messenger Faith, I ask your energy to join with mine and light my way. Allow your presence to help me to begin to give up control, to find a safe way to connect with my Higher Power. Help me to trust."©* His voice became shaky and he had a tear in his eye. *"What is this light messenger? How did I happen to choose this one without seeing what was written on the back?"*

"Who is your Light Messenger and what is the gift?"

"Faith, and the gift is trust. Oh"

"Let me tell you a bit more. The light messenger is a symbolic supporting personality that will accompany you during the entire process and later serve as an anchor after you leave the workshop. Five other members choose this messenger, Faith, and the gift being trust. Will the others please now read the message on the back of your symbol to the group? You all seem surprised by who you chose. Now please meet in small groups from similar messengers and discuss how this light messenger can help you in their own life. If no one is standing on your messenger, then choose a group you would like to join."

Iye shared with the group. *"I notice that the triangle is the symbol for messenger Faith. I am in recovery with AA and I use the 12 steps, and the symbol is the triangle. I need faith and trust that there is another, better path now for me. I need to trust that I can leave the state of Ego and move forward and develop my spiritual intelligence. I need to surrender."* Three other group members in his group shared that they were also in recovery from an addiction and were renewing their faith in a power greater than themselves.

Rita began to share. *"I am looking for truth and clarity for who I really am, I am tired of feeling unlovable. I am having problems with intimacy with my husband and want to get closer to him. I keep him at a distance. When I was a child I was abused and even though I have a lot of counseling I still am having trouble. I was married before to an abusive man and was divorced. My husband is a wonderful man and I do not want to continue to hurt him."*

"I see you chose the Light Messenger "Truth" and the gift is Clarity." She nodded. "Perhaps I can help clarify some points before we move forward. Those who have been abused are commonly split off from their intuition. They have learned over the years to tune out messages from their inner selves for at the time, these messages were too painful (Whitehead, 1994, p. 9). "Children who have been abused will tend to have poor boundaries and will have learned to ignore any sense of physical, emotional, or energetic (psychic) violation of these boundaries. They often are clueless when someone acts inappropriately with them, or are too timid to confront the other person." When a girl is sexually abused while the perpetrator is saying, "This is how someone shows you their love," it is not surprising that you might have grown up to attracted and tolerated abusive men as lovers. It was like someone put out your "light" and you began not to trust yourself, or "as if some instinctual energy had been extinguished" (Shengold, 1989, p. 18).

Rita began to cry. *"This is first time anyone put it like this. I can't believe I chose this messenger only by looking at the pictures."*

I went on. "Because pleasure was dangerous, later you will develop habits and resistance to make sure that certain positive life experiences never happen. In Ron Kurtz's Hakomi modality, resistance is called a "nourishment barrier" (as cited in Whitehead, 1994, p. 14). It is a special type of barrier whose purpose is to defend against the experience of having a basic need, e.g., trust in authority, intimacy with safety, a sense of personal power or agency in one's life, a sense of belonging and personal worth. As a child, you experienced not just frustration of your basic needs but betrayal of the satisfaction of these needs by caregivers."

"When I was being abused I would hear things "You are worthless. You are a dirty little tramp." Then I was promised a shopping trip as a reward.-that never happened"

"Your need for personal worth, safety, and intimacy and for a sense of personal power in your life was met with incessant promises for rewards that never materialized in return for age inappropriate responsibilities. I can see how much work you have done on yourself and commend you for welcoming situations where you will allow yourself to express your needs and try out new behaviors."

"I have learned that I cannot heal alone."

Iye looked at me and shared: *"I was married to someone who was very distant and I could not understand her. From your sharing, I can see how she kept her relationship with me emotionally superficial because she unconsciously expected betrayal. I guess that I am much the same way. "*

"Trust is the foundation of all of the doorways. Without trust, it is difficult to truly begin our spiritual journeys. Sadly, your wife eventually not only gave up any hope of satisfying her needs but blocked them out from her awareness all together. . Sadly, she arranged her life so that she could never satisfy her own needs. In fact, she trusted that she would be betrayed. This is not the type of trust we are talking about as you will see.

Let's see how the group is doing in terms of trust. Put your hand on the shoulder of the person who could play the role of your light messenger and share with them the reason for your choice. I see that the majority of the group is choosing Rita to represent the role of their light messenger. Everyone else has at least one hand on another person's shoulders except for Bill and Colleen. How do you both feel about not being chosen?"

Bill: *"I expected it-this always happens. I am never chosen-I really feel like people do not like me* (his eyes began to tear) *but I choose you Iye because to play the role of my light messenger because I do need to have more faith in myself and trust in others. I think you could help me."*

Colleen: *"I really did not want to be chosen to be responsible for anyone. I am always too responsible and it was a relief not to be*

*chosen. It was nice to choose you, Rita, and I chose you because I also
need clarity in my life."*

Rita: *"I am surprised that you all have such faith and trust in me
to help you. I feel that we can all go on now instead of becoming lost
in resignation and despair."*

"The Buddha said, *Faith is the beginning of all good things.*
Many of us had horrible moments of suffering in life but it is faith that
enables us to try again, to trust again, and to love again."

Rita led us into the second doorway. We were on our way.

Chapter Ten

> *"The period of greatest gain in knowledge and experience is the*
>
> *most difficult period in one's life." Dalai Lama*

The Challenge of Door Two: Truth

The Gift: Clarity

"Now we have arrived at door two, Truth. Thank you, Rita, for leading us into the second doorway of Truth. This is where we can learn to be authentic in trusting our own opinions and to release the roles that no longer serve us. The gift is clarity of our soul's mission. Part of our work in this doorway encompasses letting go of the past and understanding that our journeys have prepared us for our greater good, even though it often does not happen as we wish. In fact, many of us have found that this is the most difficult doorway."

Iye: *"I am 50 years old and I feel that I have lost so much time."*

"Don't worry about losing time because you really haven't. There are no shortcuts in life. Every situation and encounter in your life has brought you to where you are now and has served your soul. In this doorway, we have the opportunity and the ability to reframe transforming painful memories by re-imagining them from the soul's perspective of love and meaning. As we stand back from a situation or a problem, we get to see the bigger picture and see our problems in a wider context."

Bob: *"I have been angry with my parents for years. Do you mean that the disappointment and anger I have felt toward my father all these years has not been real?"*

"Experiences in the past block us because our fear or anger at the time distorts our perception of what happened. To transform our limiting experiences, we must bring what was then unconscious into the soul's realm through consciousness. We must change our perceptions and be willing to see things differently or we will continue to remain stuck in this doorway. It is important here to embrace our shadow side and be willing to see that letting go of our suffering, pain, old beliefs, and roles is the hardest work we will have to do, but yet it will also be the most rewarding. Here, we will be able to meet ourselves and our parents in a new way, seeing them as our spiritual teachers. The moment we do so, we will no longer be limited by our old beliefs."

Iye: *"OK, How do we do this?"*

"In the spirit of role reversal that we did earlier in doorway one, I will ask you to experience and share what you notice from another's person viewpoint. You may be asked to take the role of God, family members, friends, or individuals with whom you struggle. In order to find our unique path, it is necessary to become aware of the various unconscious aspects of the self often reflected in another. It is through the discovery, affirmation, and integration of these aspects that we will gradually move toward a higher sense of individuality (Jacobi, 1965; Jung & von Franz, 1964; Singer, 1972). Enough talk. Let's put this into action. Many of us play different roles unconsciously in a group. Put your hand on the shoulder of someone who could play the role of your father." Iye was heavily chosen. "Each of you please tell the person you chose, your reason for choosing them."

Maria: *"My father was distant and very analytical, Iye. You could play him."*

Bill: *"My father seemed fearful of my mother and I sense that energy in you, Iye."*

Mary: *"My father seemed angry to be stuck in his marriage. Iye, I think you could play that well."*

"Iye, how do you feel about hearing this? "

Iye: *"I am surprised but you know I thought I could hide who I was and I guess I can't. Much of this is true about my father. I chose you, Bill for the same reasons"*

"Now choose the person who could play the role of your mother and share your reasons with the person you chose. I see that Colleen you had the most hands on your shoulder. How are you experiencing this choice by the group?"

Colleen: *"It seems that I could play most people's mothers as they see an underlying anger in me. I was not chosen before to be anyone's light messenger and now I am amazed that so many hands are on me to represent the angry mother of the group. I chose you, Bill, because I sense the same kind of underlying anger in you that my own mother had!"*

"Much of this is called transference. This appears when we see in another, a representation of someone from our past history. As we continue on with the workshop and pass through the doorways, our old roles will change, and dissolve. Therefore, our choices among the group members will be different."

Our Spiritual Teachers

"Now, put your hand on the shoulder of the person who could play you. Most of the hands are on Bill's shoulders. Now after you have shared your reasons for your choices, I would like to invite you, Bill, to demonstrate how we can change our perceptions of our parents with the group." (Bill agreed) "What is your profession, Bill?"

Bill: *"I am a doctor specifically a plastic surgeon. I have a very successful practice with my own surgical center. I love my work and my staff and I love donating my time to people who have had disfiguring accidents".*

"Bring to mind a situation in which you can recall a past experience that might have made you angry with your mother and father. Now choose someone to be your parents and call them forth."

Bill: *"That's easy. I choose Iye to be my father and Colleen to represent my mother."*

"Iye and Colleen are you willing to play these roles?" (They both agreed)

"Speak to you father about your experience as a child in your family." (Bill speaks to Iye as his father.)

"I am so angry at you because you always hid behind the newspaper and would not confront my mother. You let her control us all with her drinking and affairs. You would avoid any confrontation by disappearing or sleeping. When she provoked you, you would just leave, go to work or go to sleep. You were never present for me my brother or sister, but enabled mom to keep drinking. Since mom was always drinking, we never knew what state she would be in when we came home from school. Sometimes she would be passed out on the floor and I would have to help her and protect the others. Other times, she would scream at us and call us pests and ugly children and monsters. Our house was always a mess and you never cared how it looked. I was ashamed to bring people over. I would leave the house and go find friends to play with or go to their houses, but would never stay long because I was fearful for what would happen at home. I

never wanted to be home but was afraid to not to be and even gave up playing sports after school. I would fanaticize how life would be when I was old enough to get married and have children. I swore I would never be like you. I would never be unconscious to what was going on in my own home. I would be a good father ever present for my children. I would never let anyone experience this type of pain in their family. I hated you and yet loved you. I just wanted you to be involved with me." (He began to cry.)

"Are you a good father Bill?"

Bill: *"Yes. I have three children and a wonderful wife. I do things with them all the time and we really enjoy each other. People often praise me for being a good father."*

"Who taught you how to be so present for them?"

"Not my father?"

"Yes, sometimes the worst tyrants are our best teachers. During your childhood, your soul was attempting to gain some kind of mastery or skill, but we didn't know that at the time. What did this teach you?"

Bill: *"How to be present for my family? How to be a good father? How to be involved?"*

"How long have you been angry with him?"

Bill: *"40 years."*

"Has he suffered enough?"

"He does not even know how I feel."

"I bet your office staff, friends and family always say that you help them to feel important by being involved and present for them."

"Yes, all the time. My patients tell me that all the time. They know I am involved in their medical recovery."

"Helping others to feel important and visible is a wonderful spiritual gift that we all strive for. Your father gave you that very gift by in effect not giving it to you. You can now see how this spiritual gift is very necessary in your life and career. In order to be a great plastic surgeon you really need to be present for your patients, involved and interested in their recovery. In other words you must help them to feel validated, visible and important."

"This is true. I tell my patients that surgery alone will not make them feel better about themselves but they must first feel important on the inside. I make sure they get counseling before they begin any procedure."

"Can you thank him now for the gift he gave you of teaching you how to be present for others?"

"You are kidding?" (He looked at me suspiciously.)

"What is the main way you said you would never be like him?"

"I would be present and involved with my family."

"When we get a gift and do not like the donor, what do we do with that gift? "

"Give it to others? Like I got a horrible shirt and I gave it to someone at work who just loved it."

"That's right. We give the most precious gift away that we get from our parents as fast as we can to everyone but ourselves. We never give it to ourselves. In your case, you do not really value yourself internally and often second guess yourself. When you do this it is difficult to be present for yourself.

"That is right!"

"You help others to value themselves and to feel important by being involved and present for them in fact you give away your spiritual gifts to everyone else but yourself. It is like operating from an empty bank account. Eventually you will need to replenish the funds. Now it is time to learn to value and be present for yourself."

Bill: *"I can't believe you said that. This is how come I came here! I do not feel worthwhile or important inside. I disassociate all the time and run away from my own feelings. I find I can never stay present with myself. It is easy to help others feel important. I was so afraid of becoming like my dad."*

"So maybe it is time to accept the gift from your father for yourself. A gift is never truly received without thanking the donor."

"I really need to do this?"

"This is up to you. How long have you been angry with yourself?"

He looked at me and said: *"Too long. Thank you Dad, that you never made me feel important and that you were never present for me. You taught me how to be present for others and how to help them feel important and visible. Now I am going to take the time for myself to realize that I can be present for myself and that I am important."* (With tears).

"Good. Let's look at the gift you received from your mother. Are you OK to go on? I notice you are sweating."

"I am afraid of taking everyone else's time. Oops! Let me change that. I am important enough to do this. I want to stay present for myself."

"Good. You are already accepting the gift. Now, talk to your mother."

Bill: (to Colleen standing in the role of his mother.) *"You were always drunk and loud and embarrassing to all of us. Our house was a mess and we could never have people over. You always caused scenes. You were always loud when you were awake so we never could sleep peacefully. Other times, I would come home from school and you would be passed out on the floor and no one could wake you up. We were afraid you died. Sometimes I was so angry that I wish you did. When you were awake, you would yell at me all the time and tell me how ugly I was, how I looked like a monster, how nobody would ever want me and how I ruined your life. You never wanted me. I felt worthless and like I never belonged."*

"What is your career that you love?"

"I really love the surgery I do. I volunteer to help deformed and disfigured people become whole and look good again so they can feel that they belong and feel good about themselves, I feel then like I have made a difference."

"Who taught how to do you this?"

"Oh, Now I have to thank her for making me feel worthless and ugly. Thank her for what she did not give me?"

"It's a start. How many people have thanked you for making them feel worthwhile again and not ugly. How many have thanked you for helping them feel like they belonged in society?"

"A lot and I really feel their love."

"So you did get a wonderful spiritual gift."

"Yes"

"How worthwhile and beautiful do you feel inside?"

"Not very. Sometimes I don't feel confident or accepted and still feel like that ugly child who felt like he was a monster. So I do not give this gift to myself?"

"You are getting it. It is a wonderful gift to help others feel beautiful, worthwhile, and accepted. Would you thank the person who taught you this gift? This is so you can receive it for yourself instead of giving it away."

Speaking to Colleen playing the role of his mother: *"I never wanted to make others feel as ugly and unaccepted as you make me feel; yet I can thank you for teaching me how to help others not suffer but to feel good about themselves, feel beautiful, accepted, and self confident. I love my work. In fact I want to go to more places and volunteer. I know what it is like to feel like a monster."*

"Now tell her one way that you are going to give this gift to yourself."

"I am going learn to accept and value myself and realize my own beauty. I was afraid of becoming an alcoholic like you and yet my wife told me that I have begun to drink too much as a way to be able to accept myself."

"So to sum this up, what are your spiritual gifts?"

"Now I have two spiritual gifts from my parents: from my mother the gift of acceptance and from my father the gift of being present and helping others to feel visible and important."

"I would say that these are very precious gifts; ones that we all strive for. These are necessary qualities needed to be a great plastic surgeon. When you learn to truly give these two gifts to yourself, then they are truly yours. When you can re-imagine your wounds from the perspective of the soul, (showing its higher purpose), you can see how our parents became our spiritual teachers. Thank you for your work Bill. This was very brave and I am sure it helped the entire group."

Iye: *"In the role of your father, I understood a bit more about my own father and how he would escape his marriage through logic and words. Thank you so much for helping me. I have been in this role myself."*

Colleen: *"In the role of your mother, I just did not want to deal with life. I can now understand my own mother better who was just like your mother. She got pregnant and married my father early in life and became an alcoholic. She would say I ruined her life. As a child, I always felt responsible for her and felt that I had to make something up to her for ruining her life. No wonder I was glad when the group did not choose me initially to be a light messenger. Thank you so much for giving me the opportunity to play her-now I can see the gifts she gave me. I do help others to feel wanted."*

"Let's now all come out of our roles and share what you related to in Bill's drama with Bill. When we are finished, please meet with your partner and share the spiritual gifts that you received from your parents."

(After Lunch)

"Let's check in with Bill now that we have had a good break and some rest. How are all of you feeling?"

Bill: *"I am exhausted and yet I feel so alive and free. I guess the best word is unfrozen. Can you talk a bit about what happened?"*

"What happened here was active role play. Psychodrama is a tool designed to use our energies toward experiencing the deeper meanings in behavior. Moreno (1971) referred to this as action insight. This is experiential learning at its best. In psychodrama, the abstract and unconscious becomes concrete; the psyche is experienced kinesthetically, and viscerally. The complex activities of the psyche are externally exhibited and re-created. To physically interact with these facets of the self is a powerful tool in gaining awareness, releasing emotion, and finding clarity. Active role play requires using the entire self to fully re-experience the drama in the moment. Rather than simply talking about feelings as though they were a detached part of yourself, you are able to experience your feelings in the moment as revealed in your gestures, tone of voice, and choice of words, physical stance, or other verbal and nonverbal behavior. As a result, repressed conflicts are uncovered and worked through toward a corrective reframe. Moreover, rather than talking about a childhood trauma involving your mother you had the opportunity to become the hurt child, with group members playing the roles of your mother and father. You spoke directly to your parents in the re-enactment and fully experienced the internal conflicts. By fully experiencing the trauma, you got to relive the pain, release it, find resolution, and gain a deeper understanding of yourself and in this case your parents. This allows for acceptance and integration of parts of your personality that may have been denied or disowned during childhood trauma, or your shadow side."

Bill: *"This is called our shadow? I spent my life trying not to be like my parents and then sometimes would feel myself becoming them."*

"Yes or your dark side. When you were able to see your parents as your spiritual teachers, thoughts and feelings were reframed based upon corrective experiences."

Rita: *"Your whole face seems to glow and looks so relaxed."* (The others nodded in agreement.)

"When you released the energy of long untapped feelings, the awareness and full expression of previously repressed feelings expanded your self-concept. Now you can reclaim the once disowned aspects of the self. This doorway is where we experience the positive use of adversity. We can learn and grow from our mistakes, setbacks, and suffering. Personal growth is the process of responding positively to change. Whatever comes your way, give it meaning and transform it into something of value. A precious stone cannot be polished without friction, nor humanity perfected without trials.

So, let us each look at the main thing that we wanted from our parents that we did not get." Iye raised his hand.

"I wanted privacy and respect from my mother. I do give that to others and in fact I am often praised for that. So I should thank my mother for this gift?"

"Only if you can begin to give it to yourself first."

Iye: *"I have lost my self-respect. I respect others but not myself. At the same time, I wanted attention, involvement, and direction from my father. He always seemed to be drifting off somewhere. I am present for others but not for myself. Often I disassociate from my feelings."*

"You are getting it. Curiously, the things we lacked in childhood can become the gifts we are able to give others, skills that prepare us for our life's work. Gifts that we can compassionately give to others often come from what we lacked as children, from our wounds. We often are unable to integrate these gifts into our own heart because we resist the donor or how the gifts were given. We gladly give away our gifts to others as fast as we can, without ever accepting them first into our own hearts. One way to accept them is to move past the negativity and resistance we have of refusing to forgive or by insisting that the other change for us and become the parent we wanted. Later, you will see they were just who you needed them to be."

Bob: *"This explains a lot. I am often accused of having a huge wall. I would like to break it down and truly be able to stop drinking."*

"Which light messenger did you choose?"

"Compassion. And the gift is forgiveness."

This is the next doorway. One of the symptoms of a traumatic childhood is "self medication with drugs or alcohol"(VanderKolk, 1987) or other addictive substances or behaviors. "Though these synthetic solutions may effectively quell your inner storm, in the long run, they create a bigger one" (Dayton, 2000,). Actually trauma can help us to grow and have positive outcomes from overcoming adversity. Typically posttraumatic growth is associated with positive religious coping, religious openness, and readiness to face existential questions, religious participation, and intrinsic religiousness (Shaw et al., 2005). Posttraumatic growth is manifested in an increased appreciation for life and in general, more meaningful interpersonal relationships, an increased sense of personal strength, changed priorities, and a richer existential and spiritual life (Tedeschi & Calhoun, 2004). Tedeschi and Calhoun (1996) developed the Posttraumatic Growth Inventory to measure the positive or negative changes resulting from traumatic experience. Five separate domains were identified; New Possibilities, Relating to Others, Personal Strength, Appreciation for Life, and Spiritual Change. An individual may experience growth in one or more domains, while experiencing no change or negative change in others.

Success with efforts to repair traumatic childhoods leads to a certain emotional stick-to-itiveness in the face of adversity which is at the heart of resilience (Fonagy et al., 1994). You certainly have all become resilient in your lives and this is a gift. Being able to reframe what has happened to you will lead to increased clarity as well as to more confidence in your own abilities, and trust in the capacity of others to respond (Tronick, 1989).

We have now learned the truth about how come we had the parents we did. We are also beginning to become clear about the gifts we received from them that are needed for our higher purpose. Realize that you have choices in life. You can choose to be content with who you are now or accept the gifts you have rejected for so long and move forward. Adversity is our teacher. When we view adversity as a guide towards greater inner growth, we will then learn to accept the wisdom our soul came into this life to learn.

Now are now ready to leave our Rational Intelligence (What I Think) and move on to our Emotional Intelligence (What I Feel) and go through doorways three and four accompanied with the gifts each of you earned of trust and clarity."

> "Letting go of our suffering is the hardest work we will ever do. It is also the most fruitful. To *heal* means to meet ourselves in a new way -- in the newness of each moment where all is possible and nothing is limited to the old."
>
> *Steven Levine (1998)*

Chapter Eleven

> *"The great pleasure and feeling in my right brain is more than my left brain can find the words to tell you."* Roger Sperry -Nobel Prize Winner (1961)

Emotional Intelligence: Bridging the Gap

We are now ready to enter doorways three, compassion; and door four, love. Our emotional intelligence bridges the gap between the left and right brain and also between our rational and spiritual intelligences. A friend of mine, Ivo Banaco from Portugal, said: *"Like me, other boys and girls, men and women could access all the information that they want. If we have a problem, let's find it in Google! It's like a big manual of instructions that seems to have all the solutions for all the problems. And what is the Souldrama main message? All this rational information simply is not enough! It is important but is not sufficient. The cognitive intelligence creates an important space to go deeper into the emotional and to the soul. But you will not get these last two lines of development in Google, you only get it through direct experience, to allow yourself to be touched, to suffer, to smile, to be vulnerable...to feel."*

Iye : *"Where does this expression "EI" come from? I sometimes feel emotionally illiterate. Is that what EI stands for, emotional illiteracy?"*

"No Iye. It stands for Emotional Intelligence. Point to yourself."

Iye: *"OK"*(Points)

"To where did you just point?"

"To my heart"

"Notice that you did not point to your head! This is Emotional Intelligence."

Lisa: *"I often "know" one thing and "feel" another. Many times I ignore my heart and go with my head and I am often accused in work of being rigid."*

"A world without emotions is robotic and dead. Emotional intelligence helps us to put words to feelings and helps us to understand what is occurring inside and outside of us. Many of know that when it comes to making decisions, feelings count even more than our thoughts. Our rational intelligence holds no value without considering our emotions. Emotional Intelligence is often measured as an Emotional Intelligence Quotient (EQ), describing an ability, capacity, or skill to perceive, assess, and manage the emotions of one's self, of others, and of groups. In Souldrama, we use the concept of Emotional Intelligence to stand for "what I feel." Since this is a relatively new area of psychological research, the definition of EI is constantly changing.

All emotions are impulses to act, in fact the very word, emotion comes from the Latin root "motere" to move plus the prefix "e" which means to move away, suggesting a inclination to act is contained in every emotion. Even though the term was first used early in the 1900's, the field is growing rapidly. In 1940, David Wechsler described the influence of non-intellective factors on intelligent behavior, and argued that our models of intelligence would not be complete until we could adequately describe these factors. In 1983, Howard Gardner's *Frames of Mind: The Theory of Multiple Intelligences* introduced the idea of Multiple Intelligences which included both *Interpersonal intelligence* (the capacity to understand the intentions, motivations, and desires of other people) and *Intrapersonal intelligence* (the capacity to understand oneself, to appreciate one's feelings, fears, and motivations). Throughout our workshop, we have been using psychodrama to deal with our intrapersonal relationships and sociometry to deal with our interpersonal relationships.

Gardner was primarily interested in approaching students with diverse learning potentials. He believed that traditional types of intelligence, such as IQ, fail to fully explain cognitive ability. He encouraged educators and scientists to place a greater emphasis on the search for multiple intelligences. Thus, even though the names given to the concept varied, there was a common belief that traditional definitions of intelligence were lacking in ability to fully explain performance outcomes. I personally like the first published attempt made by Salovey and Mayer (1990) who defined EI as "the ability to monitor one's own and others' feelings and emotions, to discriminate among them and to use this information to guide one's thinking and actions This definition was later revised to "The ability to perceive emotion, integrate emotion to facilitate thought, understand emotions, and to regulate emotions to promote personal growth ".(Mayer & Salovey, 1997)"

Carlo: "I just read a book by Daniel Goleman, "Emotional Intelligence: Why It Can Matter More Than IQ". Is this where the term became widely popularized?"

"In his groundbreaking book, Goleman (1995) articulated the kind of intelligence that our hearts, or emotions, have. Further, Goleman used brain and behavioral research to show how come people with high IQ's can flounder with emotions and those with a modest IQ's can do very well. Some of the factors that added up to a different way of being "smart" included self discipline, self-awareness, and empathy. Emotional Intelligence is a sense of knowing where people are coming from. While childhood is a critical time for its development, emotional intelligence is not fixed at birth and can be developed, nurtured, and strengthened throughout adulthood with immediate benefits to our work and relationships. These following competencies are not innate talents, but rather learned capabilities that must be worked on and developed to achieve outstanding performance. He suggests that individuals are born with a general emotional intelligence and that determines their potential for learning emotional competencies. Goleman's model also includes skills that drive managerial performance. His model outlines four main constructs for EI. For our purposes:

- Self-awareness - the ability to read one's emotions and recognize their impact while using gut feelings to guide decisions. This is where we can use our intuition.

- Self-management - involves controlling one's emotions and impulses and adapting to changing circumstances. This involves being flexible, open minded, and being able to put ourselves in another's shoes.

- Social awareness - the ability to sense, understand, and react to other's emotions while comprehending social networks. This involves having compassion and celebrating diversity.

- Relationship management - the ability to inspire, influence, and develop others while managing conflict and maintaining love for self and others.

These can easily be incorporated into the action model of Souldrama as we go through the third and fourth doors. In doorways three and four the emotional competencies we want to develop are compassion and love."

"How come we do not learn this when we are growing up?" asked Maria.

"How did you learn to communicate and regulate your emotions in your family?"

Maria: *"By slamming doors on the way out of the house or by silence for days at a time."*

Iye: *"By silence for days and then pretending nothing was wrong."*

"Our parents teach us about relationships. Virginia Satir said "Once a human being has arrived on this earth, communication is the largest single factor determining what kinds of relationships he makes with others and what happens to him in the world about him." What did you learn by watching your parents?"

Rita: *"I learned that relationships cannot be trusted."*

Doug: *"Wow, I learned that they are not talked about. In my family, we never talked about feelings even when my sister died. I never even had the chance to decide and reflect about how I felt. I feel like I have been operating on automatic pilot ever since."*

"Dr. Tian Dayton (2008) includes ideas on how to attain emotional literacy--the skill of translating feelings into words so that we can use our thought processes to understand and bring our emotions into balance, as well as how to calm the limbic system so that we can actually experience what we're feeling. She states that "If emotions are not talked about in families, children will later have a difficult time identifying and communicating their emotions. Self reflection is limited and there is a lack of awareness about why they do what they do, or why they feel what they feel. They may be all action with little awareness of what is driving their behaviors or what is going on underneath." (Dayton, 2005)

Bob: *"The chaos in my family was so great that I began to drink at an early age."*

Iye: *"I really have a difficult time putting my feelings into words."* The others nodded.

"Let's do a little more sociometry. Let's all stand up. I invite you to put your hand on the shoulder of someone that you would like to have join you for dinner. I see that most of the hands are on Lisa's shoulder. Share one by one the reason for your choice. I notice that some of you are not chosen. How do you feel about this?"

Donald: *"Left out as usual."*

"Thank you both for sharing. What would you like to be chosen for, Donald?"

Donald: *"I would like the group to know that I love to take hikes in nature and I would like people to ask me for advice where to go."*

"How do you feel about being chosen Lisa?"

Lisa: *"I am honored. I didn't think anyone even noticed me."*

Bob: *"I chose you Lisa because I thought you would be a good listener."*

Iye to Colleen: *"I did not choose you to have dinner with but I would choose you to go to the beach with. I am afraid of the water and I believe you could help me. I would feel safe with you."*

"So you see each person is chosen for different criteria. As children, we did not have very many choices, nor did we have the luxury of expressing them in a healthy environment. Here in group, we can do that. Here our choices and preferences become visible. Let's try this again. Now put your hand on the shoulder of the person you would most like to help you with your math homework. I see most of the hands are on your shoulder, Iye."

"I am surprised that I am chosen without the group even knowing a lot about me!"

"Now please sit in pairs and answer these questions. Were you afraid you would not be chosen so you chose someone first or did wait to be chosen and not take a risk to move? What would you like to be chosen for by the group?"

What Are You Really Saying?

"Dr. Dayton said, "Being able to attach words to feeling states is a corner stone of developing emotional literacy and consciously regulating behavior. We need to think about what we are feeling in order to understand what is occurring inside and outside of us and to use that understanding to regulate our thinking, feeling and behavior. Physical gestures and actions for young children become double coded with emotional meaning. Emotional learning is a mind/body phenomenon. The limbic system which is the brain body system that is associated with the regulation of our psychological and emotional states can become deregulated in individuals who grow up in less than optimal environments. Emotional deregulation can lead to anything from moodiness to depression to acting out behaviors such as bullying, violence and addiction." (Dayton, Internet, 2009)

Maria:" I never know what I am feeling and my husband always says that he cannot keep up with my feelings. He said it's like living on a roller coaster. I am Italian and we use a lot of hand gestures so he said he had to learn to read sign language!"

"The body is always silently speaking. Addiction in a family can cause emotional imbalance that leads to both personal and familial imbalance. When primary caregivers consistently allow a child to be over-stimulated or grossly under-stimulated, as can be the case in homes where relationship trauma is present, the child may not learn how to develop an affective range of emotions. Instead of being able to regulate emotions, these individuals may bounce from one emotional extreme to another." (Dayton, 2005)

So think about growing up. "Gesturing or action is our first language. It is the mind-body, communication upon which all subsequent language is built. Before language formally enters the picture, we have learned a rich tapestry of gestures and actions to communicate our needs and desires. This gesturing comprises a nonverbal communication that informs our ability to express ourselves and understand others throughout our lives." (Dayton, 2009)

"All of this body language is part and parcel of an action oriented, gestural communication and contains important connotation. Each tiny gesture is double coded with emotion and is stored by the brain and body with emotional purpose and meaning attached to it. Through this interactive process of communicating our needs and desires, we build emotional intelligence and literacy as surely as we learn math in a classroom. Because gesturing is our first form of communication, much of this language becomes part of our unconscious and surfaces in the form of "automatic emotion". (Dayton, 2009)

Iye: *"This is like sending information or e mails from one computer to another!"*

"Yes, all this information gets sent very quickly! Non verbal connections are very important and they show what we understand about another. "Significant information gets transferred from one system to another, but it happens, in what feels like, an invisible realm." (Dayton, Internet 2009) "Let me show you the cover of the New Yorker magazine."

McGuire / The New Yorker; © Condé Nast Publications.

This is a beautiful representation of how we communicate non verbally. Dayton goes on to say " Many people particularity if they have had a lack of this gestural form of communication or have grown up in environments where feelings were not talked about have a hard time identifying some of their emotions and their intentions when they try to self reflect. They have a lack of awareness about why they do what they do, or why they feel, what they feel. They may be all action with little awareness of what is driving their behaviors or what is going on underneath. Or perhaps they experience something in their body, like chronic muscle stiffness or pain in their stomach, back or head, but they are unable to make any connections as to emotional feelings that may be being somatized rather than felt. They may misread or not pick up on the subtle signals from others that are a part of non verbal communication." (Dayton, 2005)

"Clare: *I often get stomach pains when things become too intense!*"

"I like to say that if you don't scream, your body will:"

"Other symptoms of living with chronic stress are depression, sleep problems, apathy, and isolation as well as moodiness and acting out behaviors such as bullying, violence and addiction" (Dayton, 2008) Let's stand up again. Please put your hand on the shoulder of someone who you think really "gets you".

I noticed that Clare, who had not spoken up much during group, was heavily chosen. She began to cry. "Share with one another how come you chose them."

Clare: *"I am very surprised. I did not think people even noticed me".*

"Carlo, I see you were not chosen."

Carlo: *"I am not surprised as I often keep myself from others. I like to be the observer. I feel better just talking about this and in doing so feel heard and seen."*

"We all want to be seen and heard. This is something we were supposed to receive in our families. For a few days, set an intention to be aware of your communication styles and skills. How do you typically communicate? Is it through words, gestures, emotions, thoughts, desires, needs, truths, direct perception, or intuition? Do you focus more on the other person or on yourself? Do you typically tell, ask or listen? Do you shut others down and do you always need to be right? If you aren't sure, others can probably tell you in a group situation." Iye looked embarrassed.

After you've spent some time talking with someone, reflect on what your underlying motives were and what level of depth you reached. Write your insights in your journal. This exercise will help you become more aware and conscious of who you are and why you do what you do. We need to have people in our lives where we can be as open as possible and take the risk to tell them how we feel." Iye looked embarrassed.

Iye: *"I know you chose me to help me with your math homework however, I don't know if you would trust me to share your feelings."*

Emotional **Sobriety**

"I congratulate you on your vulnerability, Iye. Emotional Sobriety is a term coined by Bill Wilson a founder of Alcoholics Anonymous, when he was discussing spirituality."

Iye: *"I am very familiar with Bill W."* Others nodded.

"I think that many oldsters who have put our AA to severe but successful tests still find they often lack emotional sobriety. Perhaps they will be the spearhead for the next major development in AA – the development of much more real maturity and balance (which is to say humility) in our relations, with ourselves, with our fellows and with God. Thus, I think it can work out with emotional sobriety. If we examine every disturbance we have, great or small, we will find at the root of it some unhealthy demand. Let us, with God's help, continually surrender these hobbling demands. Then we can be set free to live and love. We may then be able to 12th Step others and ourselves into emotional sobriety" (Wilson).

"When a family lives in chaos "Children cannot flee, where would they go? They cannot fight, they would lose. So they shut down, they freeze, they flee on the inside. But without somehow processing what's going on for them, that numbed and frozen pain can live within the self system, an emotional accident waiting to happen, in what is now called a *post traumatic stress reaction*. That is what being an ACOA (Adult Child of Trauma and Addition) is all about. Years after the stressor is removed, the ACOA lives as if it is still there. As if some emotional threat, lurks just around the corner. "This is the dilemma of the adult child of either addiction or trauma. Unresolved pain from childhood gets recreated and acted out in adult relationships" (Dayton, 2008).

People, who have experienced dysfunctional parents, tend to select and continue to select partners that essentially resonate with their parents in some way and that in the end are not good for them. In other words, we become loyal to their dysfunction or to our parents worst traits."

Bill: *"Well half a relationship was always better than none for me!"*

"Our early emotional experiences imprint long-lasting patterns into the very fabric of our brain's neural networks and in order to bridge the gap we need a therapy that takes into account our emotional intelligence (Lewis et al., 2001). Psychotherapy, helps to change our patterns just enough to allow the person to begin to select more comfort-inducing partners and friends. Humans are never able to be "independent", we have a permanent need for connection with others. I think many schools of psychotherapy are moving in the direction of acknowledging how important connections and relationships are. It is important to extend this also to global connections (Lewis, 2001)."

Mary: *How come men seem to isolate more that women during stressful times?*

"Males and females respond to stress differently. In general, female responses to stress are to "tend and befriend," whereas male responses are to "fight or flight" (Taylor et al., 2000). Traumatized girls tend to sacrifice themselves in return for the connection with others that is so vitally important. Traumatized boys tend to prefer avoidance and emotional distance, sacrificing the connection with others in return for the illusion of autonomy. In recent research on women's use of one another to reduce stress and in reaction to external difficulties, it is demonstrated that this leads to less stress hormones than are found in men in reaction to for example, job stressors. While men tend to withdraw, isolate, and suffer from a surge of stress hormones, women congregate and bond. It is suggested that this may lead to longer lives, as well as to more immediate comfort to say nothing of less stress related neurochemistry (Lewis, 2001)."

Bill: *"You know, I am so glad you are telling me this because I always thought I was crazy."*

Iye: *"That's me. Growing up, I could only feel like I could be myself when I was alone."*

Where Did You Just Go?

Bill: *"I am having a hard time right now sitting and listening to everyone's feelings."*

Iye: *"I noticed that Bill said he often dissociates-I do too. What is that about?"*

"Let's talk a bit about dissociation. Dissociation is a normal response to trauma. It is an unexpected partial or complete break of a person's thoughts, memories, feelings, actions, or sense of identity; in other words, the normal incorporation of a person's conscious functioning. It stops us from being fully present as it allows the mind to distance itself from experiences that are too painful.

Different dissociative disorders that are related to stress and trauma are PTSD, dissociation, somatization, and inappropriate affect (Van Kolk, 1996). These symptoms often occur together. The treatment of dissociative symptoms may be most effective when it supports the cognitive/emotional processing of trauma-related material and encourages the development of greater affect regulation capacities (Briere, 2006)."

Bob: *"It is difficult for me to be able to stay happy too long. I always feel like the other shoe is going to drop!"* "If we do not process our emotional pain, we later become hyper vigilant –always on the lookout for what could happen. We develop many ways and defenses to keep us safe, including walls. Suppose for example, you are all feeing safe here in the group room. One day I tell you that there is a bomb on the property that could go off at any moment. We would always be on edge protecting ourselves so not to be hurt. This protection also stops us later from receiving the love we all so desperately need."

Some of the group piped up.

Iye: *"Yes and when I go home for the holidays I am lucky if I can reach the doorknob when I leave- I feel so small. I have been accused of having walls."*

Dissociation is "the escape when there is no escape" (Putnam, 1992, p.104). If you have been brought up with trauma, the body can't tell the difference between an emotional emergency and physical danger. Dr Dayton states that "we do what we can as children; we freeze and shut down our inner responses by numbing or fleeing on the inside through dissociating. We learn over time to close down our emotions and to deny and reject our authentic feelings losing valuable information that would help us to function well later in our relational world." (Dayton, 1995)Lisa: *"My sister helped calm me but I really wanted my parents."*

Iye: *"Yes and I had my dog.* (With a tear in his eye) *I always cuddled him."*

Bob: *"I felt so helpless in my family."*

"Sadness is painful. You learned to hide what we were really feeing and felt bad that you could not fix it. Now you will learn new responses so you no longer respond from fear. It is important to feel our sadness as well, for when we do we discharge this old energy and can heal our emotional pain."

"So why can't we just sit here and talk about things instead of acting them out? said Bill. *How can action methods help?"*

Don't Tell Me, Show Me!

"If we sit here and just talk about things, our feelings will later be acted out in relationships. J.L. Moreno (1971) that believed that what was learned in action must be unlearned in action and what was learned in relationship must be unlearned in relationship. The goal in therapy is always to access our spontaneity and creativity to undo old roles and patterns of thinking, feeling and behaving and relearning new, more adequate ways of experiencing and expressing the self in a relational context. Action methods allow us to express our pain creatively and symbolically.

Action methods allow us to enter the therapeutic setting and then words can follow. We can first experience ourselves in action, and then decode our experience with words; i.e. we can learn the skills of emotional literacy." (Dayton, 2005)

Lisa: *"So we need to integrate our RQ and EQ?"*

"Yes, it is important to be able to balance and put words to our feelings."

George spoke up: " *I am afraid that I will do all this work and feel on top of the world and come back to my same environment and get sucked right back into the same situation.*"

"Yes, George and sometimes we will go home and find that our workplace is not much different than our family of origin. By developing our emotional intelligence here at this workshop, you will lean new tools that will allow you to express yourself and your choices more clearly.

As Greenspan (1997) said, "Emotional development is not just the foundation for important capacities such as intimacy and trust. It is also the foundation of intelligence and a wide variety of cognitive skills. At each stage of development, emotions lead the way, and learning facts and skills follow."

> *"It is in the space between inner and outer world, which is also the space between people--the transitional space--that intimate relationships and creativity occur." Winnicott." -1951-*

Chapter Twelve

> *"The most pathetic person in the world is the person who has sight, but no vision."*
>
> *Helen Keller*

Vision Boards: Seeing Your Soul in Action

"Einstein said that, "Your imagination is your preview to life's coming attractions." We use vision boards in Souldrama to help us to see our soul in action. Actually one of the stages necessary to develop emotional literacy includes being able to visualize images, ideas and symbols according to Stanley Greenspan.(1997) This is the stage of true symbolic expression when we begin to deal not only with behavior but with ideas, understanding that one thing can stand for another, that an image of something can represent the thing itself. This realization allows us to create an inner picture of our world. Moreover, these symbols (i.e. mental pictures, gestures, feeling states, or words) can represent not only our own intentions, wishes, and feelings, but those of other people as well.

Our Souls Intention

Now we are going to take some time to make our vision boards. Let me talk about these for a while. We have been making these with every Souldrama workshop and now I have at least seven boards. They have all come true. I had to stop making them because I could not keep up with the energy of my own soul in action."

Colleen: *"What are vision boards for?"*

"Our soul speaks in terms of vision and not words. When we make a vision board, it is the soul speaking to us reminding us of how we can nourish ourselves by giving ourselves what we did not get from our parents. This is often reflected in the vision of the spiritual gifts we give to others.

When we make vision boards, we are putting down our soul's intention. If you can see it then it can exist, and if you passionately believe in something that has not yet come into existence, you can create it. We hold the power to create whatever we desire. Our ability to manifest the changes we desire depends on the depth and passion of our beliefs and on the focus of our attention. "

Maria: *Like it says in the Bible "As you think, so shall you be."*

"Yes, Maria. You cannot envision what you cannot experience. With this understanding, we, as individuals and as society, can design a whole new future for ourselves. Our challenge is to break free of society's world view, to truly empower our imaginations to create brand new realities. This brings a whole new meaning to 'vision.' -- Louisa May Alcott (year) said it well "Far away there in the sunshine are my highest aspirations. I may not reach them, but I can look up and see their beauty, believe in them, and follow where they lead."

"When we say we are going to do something, we set energy in motion. When we fail to act or complete our intention, we drain our energy. We lose our power. Therefore, we would be wise to choose our words carefully -- to really mean what we say and to honor the commitments we have made. Put your intention into the present for this keeps you aware of the present moment. It also indicates trust in yourself and a higher power.

Our vision boards will represent the big picture for your life and will give a larger, purposeful, even spiritually ideal picture of where you are going. Your mind needs to have a clear and challenging vision to draw you ever upwards. I desire that you live by your imagination and not your history.

Now, I would like you to cut out some pictures from some of the magazines you brought and paste them on this poster board in any random way you like. These pictures should represent what you want in terms of your career, relationships, home, family, travel, leisure time, spirituality, health.

What do you passionately desire for your own life? For the planet? Where do you want to live? What do you want your career to look like? What do you want your relationships to look like? Let your soul speak. How much passion do you feel for your goals? Be as creative as you like as you work with them.

Have fun." (The group became loud and joyful as they made their boards and became like children cutting and pasting!)

"Now share with the group one word to describe the "essence" of your board and let's put the boards against the wall where we can view them until we are ready to work more with them during the third the level of spiritual intelligence. Look around the room and see the energy that we just created here. This is the bigger picture of your life that you created. Life plays with energy and matter to expand, create, express, and evolve. It explores new possibilities, realizes them, and then reaches for even more. Life continually transforms what is into something brand new."

> *"Every moment of your life is infinitely creative and the universe is endlessly bountiful. Just put forth a clear enough request, and everything your heart desires must come to you."* - Shakti Gawain-

Chapter Thirteen

> *"The fruit of love is service, which is compassion in action."*
>
> -Mother Theresa-

The Challenge of Door Three: Compassion

The Gift: Forgiveness

"We have now arrived at door three and will begin to bridge the gap of emotional intelligence. The gift is forgiveness as we learn to be tolerant of others, express our empathy, and celebrate diversity. We value each other for our differences not despite them."

"It is hard for me to let go of what happened in the past." said Carlo, a bodybuilder.

"Spiritual love is so full of the ideal that we must learn to embrace imperfection. We need to align the ego and soul to build spiritual muscle. In heaven where everything is already attained, there is no growth-it is through the descending and awakenings that we build spiritual muscle. Each time you go to the gym, you can hold heavier weights and keep them up longer as you build more muscle. So it is with our spirituality. This takes time and practice. Each time we forgive, we are building spiritual muscle. Spiritual muscle conditioning is critical. This is how we produce consistent results. Once again, remember that any pattern of emotional behavior that is reinforced or rewarded on a consistent basis will become conditioned and automatic. Any pattern that we fail to reinforce will eventually dissipate."

"Yes, but my sister is so mean", said Bill. *"I do not know if I can forgive her. She has hurt me so much."*

"To get forgiveness, we must first work through the painful experiences associated with it. Forgiveness does not mean someone has done something terribly wrong and now that we are so spiritually evolved we are willing to forgive. That is called judgment -- I have forgiven you, but judged you first. Metaphysical consciousness states that if I judge or attack you, I will be separate from you and will be in pain. If someone says something mean to you, is their meanness who they are? A person who was mean to you was not connected to their own love, so they judge you, and that tempts you to judge them back and then you are hurt. That person's heart was shut down and not in touch with your innocence. Therefore, they spoke to your guilt and that shut you down. In fact, guilt helps to isolate us and that feeds the ego. We use a lot of energy when we constantly blame others and this energy should be used to get on with our lives."

"I guess I do have some guilt where my sister is concerned. I used to beat her up when I was a child. I was older and did not know how to express my pain."

"All the people in our lives - the ones who bring out our strengths and the ones who bring out our weaknesses - heal us. Our relationships can be seen as assignments. They are the perfect opportunities for us to be a witness in our own life. We can either avoid or embrace this opportunity. Either way, it is important that we fully commit to each choice. Life here becomes a mirror as we learn that as Carl Jung (1978) said "Everything that irritates us about others can lead us to an understanding of ourselves."Practice forgiveness from both the aspects of the ego and the soul. What would your ego say? What would your soul say? Beliefs separate us; loving thoughts unite us, and make us one."

Bill thought about it and said *"I see the difference. My ego would say she does not know any better and my soul would say I want her to be my sister and I love her. I miss having a family."*

"Now which thought would bring you closer to her and to forgiveness? Judgment, guilt, and shame stop forgiveness. Forgiveness has to be done from the heart. Often, when we try to forgive another, it is actually ourselves we are the most resentful toward. Ask yourself who is it you won't forgive or can't forgive completely? The one who you need to forgive the most is the one you feel does not deserve it. Forgiveness is really for you, not the other person. We often spend years not forgiving, being bitter and wasting precious time. When we stay angry it is because we usually have a need that was not met."

Guilt and Control

"I wish I could forgive my ex wife." said Iye. *"I can't get over the feeling that she owes me something."*

"I know it is difficult to forgive when we are angry and hurt. I acknowledge you for honoring your feelings, for by being fully present with them helps you to release the feelings themselves. When you do not forgive, you leave the relationship with the thought that the other person "owes" you something and keep a sense of entitlement or in other words you are still blaming them for something. The ego needs you to feel guilty and unworthy in order to keep you in its limited world of the past and the future, where it is in control. Guilt and blame are the two main strategies of control. It is also the way we avoid living in true responsibility. If I can blame someone for the way I feel or what is happening in my life, I can avoid taking responsibility for myself. Someone else is to blame. If I can make someone feel guilty, it is easier to control them and have them assume responsibility for me. It is nothing but a strategy to control others and avoid responsibility for ourselves. When we live a life we are proud of, we still make mistakes. It is natural and human. If we hang onto the guilt or know that others will remain guilty we focus on the ego and this is another way that ego can control our lives."

Mary: *"I would keep trying to be who I thought my husband wanted me to be."*

"Pretending to be someone other than yourself only broadens the distance between the person you are and the one with whom you are trying to establish closeness."

"I found that out!"

"We often enter into relationships with people who trigger our childhood wounds, the places that show our character defects. They get triggered when we do not know how to adjust out of the wound. Without spiritual maturity, the same issue will be triggered over and over again. Real healing is when the energy is changed, when we honor others by not imposing our old dramas on them. If we feel that things are wrong because other people are "that way", we will never be healed. We need to shift the focus to point to a weakness that is within ourselves. Their wounds represent our wounds.

At the core of all anger is a need that is not being fulfilled. Analytical thinking is reduced when one connects with the loving energy of soul and a feeling of forgiveness often follows. When we begin to live in the present by connecting with the soul, we stop analyzing who did what to us in childhood and free ourselves from negative thinking. When we stop holding grudges, we begin to nourish the soul. When you are confused by the people around you, and frustrated by the circumstances within which you find yourself, remember that everyone and everything within your experience is a product of the circumstances out of which they have arisen."

God, You Can Have Everything In My Life, Except My Relationship. I Will Do That By Myself!

"Every relationship in your life is an experience to grow and transform your life. Choice is your greatest power; you can choose to be more loving or to forgive. Forgiveness means letting go of the past so that you can heal in the present. It is our relationship to the idea of relationships that is the problem. When we open our hearts, miracles occur. Consciousness is all about relationships, especially how the lower relates to the higher and how the darkness can exist within the light. When we reach spiritual maturity, we can hold and experience contradictions like anger with love. This is where we can let opposites coexist in us at the same time without choosing one over the other. To grow in consciousness, we must expand our perspectives on life. The purpose of relationships is transformation, not happiness!"

Iye: *"So how do we do that?"*

"The more we work with the concept of unity and wholeness, the more everything makes sense. Relationships are a challenge because life pulls us in opposite directions at the same time. Our ego feels the need to be unique and special and so our focus lies on how we are different from others. Differences hold the potential to create conflict. At the same time, our souls live through connection with others. We are challenged to rise to discover how we and the other are the same. Parts have meaning when they are understood to be parts of a bigger picture. We need to balance the two tendencies toward uniqueness and connection. Watch your reactions, responses, feelings and thoughts about other people and events. This will give you clues about your unconscious programming. Ask yourself: How do I judge or stereotype people? What pushes my buttons? What makes me angry or fearful or sad? Call your parents to mind and see what judgments come up. Now do the same with your spouse, siblings, your partner, and your children.

Look around the room, put your hand on the shoulder of the person who could play the role of someone you find the most difficult to forgive in your own personal life and share with that person how come you chose them."

Mary: "*I was chosen by Colleen to play the role of her mother because she is angry with her for ignoring her, yet Bill chose me to play his sister who died after running away from home and Carlo saw me as himself.*"

Iye: "*Carlo chose me to be the soul of his dead father who he wants to forgive for leaving him before he got to know him, Bill chose me because he wants to forgive his father for never being there and Colleen chose me because she wants to forgive her father for being so angry. So I was surprised to be seen so many different ways!*"

"Yes, everyone reacted differently based on their own perceptions and beliefs. The outer incidents that trigger these reactions in you simply mirror your own nature. If you didn't have beliefs around the issues that upset you, you would not have a reaction to a person. When outer events spark a reaction, we need to look inside to explore what's going on. Ask yourself what role could this person play in my family of origin and remember that we discover in ourselves what others hide from us and we recognize in others what we hide from ourselves.

Think about the people you work with. Perhaps they have a personality characteristic you don't like, one that touches you where you are wounded. What we need is a readiness to forgive-who do you feel the most ready to forgive? Who do you find the most difficult to forgive? Who could play these roles for you in our group? Make the goal not forgiveness but to go as far as possible in the forgiveness process in order to reduce the impact of that person on our lives. Sit together in pairs and talk about this for a few minutes."

About Bob

"Let's do some more sociometry. Stand up and put your hand on the person's shoulder who reminds you or who could play the role of someone that you feel the most ready to forgive. (Most hands went on Bob's shoulder) Share with the person you chose who this person reminds you of."

Bob: "*I chose you Iye as you remind me of my son who died when he was 13 by committing suicide. I have never talked about this for over 20 years and I would like to work on this. I don't believe I just said this!"*

"Good. Choose someone to be your son." He chose Iye.

"Let's bring him back into the room at age 13 and you can talk with him."

"OK" He began to cry, *"Today is your birthday. I am angry-furious with you for shooting yourself. You were only 13. You came home from school and you shot yourself and when we came home from work, we found you there in your room. I can never forgive you or I for letting this happen. I have spent 20 years trying to figure out what your mother and I did wrong and have done nothing but drink since you died. I have been in and out of rehabilitation hospitals and when I drink the pain is less. I have no purpose. I did not even know you were on drugs. We did everything together, hunting, fishing, and always talked about our problems. You were my best friend. Why did you not tell me you had a problem?"*

The roles were reversed and: Iye said this back to Bob in the role of his son Rob.

Bob in the role of Rob: *"I would not tell you how many drugs I was taking. I was so ashamed. You were such a good father and I could not disappoint you. I did not mean to kill myself-I was only playing with the gun and had taken drugs earlier with my friends. I wish I had told you about the drugs."*

I asked Rob: "How does it feel to see your father so depressed and unhappy for 20 years?"

Bob in the role of Rob: *"It is horrible. I feel like I have ruined his life and I wish he would find a purpose. My mother is very unhappy as she has lost both my father and me."*

"Is there a purpose that you would like to suggest to give your father's life meaning?"

Rob: *"I feel that you are trying to make us both feel guilty, Dad. My soul is in a place where I am at peace and yet I see you suffer every day, but I do not. I want to know that my life had a purpose. This is what you can do for me. Stop keeping me alive by drinking and sadness. Keep me alive by giving my life a purpose. Take other teenage boys who never had a father like you that are on drugs and show them another way of life. Do this for me and give my short time on earth a purpose. Yes, you made me your purpose when I was alive. I also had a purpose being with you and that was to teach you something. Give my life some value and meaning. You and mom did not die with me. Do this for me."*

Tears all around. Roles were reversed again.

Bob*: "I never looked at it this way...through your eyes—all I saw was my own misery and my own hurt. I will give your life a purpose and begin to help the boys in my 12 step program. I can start by taking them riding with our horses and telling them about you. I am ready to let you go and I would like to turn you over to a higher power."*

The group shared and with Bob.

Iye*:" I never knew it until lately but my father had a brother very close to him who committed suicide. Now I know how he must have felt."*

"Let's all share something with Bob about how his drama relates to your own life and then break for lunch. Thank you, Bob for having the courage to help all of us."

Walk a Mile in Another's Shoes

We just returned from lunch and the group seemed somewhat serious.

"What just happened in that drama" said Iye?

"When we view situations through the emotional lens of the past what we see is not the experience but the event within us. We often overreact to the situation through our old roles, feeding into the ego, and becoming trapped in the emotions. Instead of feeling and explaining away the pain, Bob was allowed in Door Three to totally experience the feelings and emotions right there in the "here and now" and connect with his past feelings. When we refuse to feel or want the moment to be different, we feed the ego, and we all want inner acceptance of all our feelings."

Bob*:" I feel so relieved."*

"Here you learned compassion for yourself and others and the minute you realized the pain was inside and not outside of yourself, it began to disappear. You allowed yourself to accept whatever you needed to feel and did not judge yourself."

"I feel so much closer to you, Bob", said Colleen. (The others nodded as well.)

"I am sure if I asked you to stand up and put your hand on the shoulder of the person you feel closest to now, the answer would be Bob." The group nodded.

"Moreno suggested that God is imminent, creative, and the supreme co-creator promoting respect and honor between group members. As we see the light of God in each group member we gain an understanding of the universal struggles of all humans. This encourages conscious living in each and every moment. Therefore, we are more likely to value our own uniqueness and that of others and as a consequence, one's impulse to judge or criticize diminishes (Moreno, 1972). This combination of self and other awareness moves you through the process of forgiveness as you let go of judgments and resentments."

Forgive and Forget?

"So if I forgive the person who abused me, I need to be friends with them?" asked Colleen.

"It is helpful to help people differentiate between forgiveness and reconciliation. Forgiveness can be done by the offended person and basically involves refusing to be re-victimized by continuing to stay hurt or inflaming their anger by savoring plans for revenge. Reconciliation is between two people and requires that the offender repent, make amends, or at least accept the wronged person's feelings enough to be willing to work to try heal the relationship."

"I have a hard time forgiving myself, said Iye. *I made so many mistakes and hurt my loved ones so much."*

The others nodded.

"Self-forgiveness-think of the very word! This is a word that separates us more from God. Let's change it to ego forgiveness. God is all forgiving. Every time we think we are separate from God, we think that we can control our lives. Because our lives are really the lives of God, they can really manage themselves. Rather than change ourselves, we want to change other people and the world. On some level some part of us wants to stay the same. Spiritual growth is about letting go of false perceptions and thoughts so that other dimensions can emerge. It is about totally shifting your identity. If we hang onto the guilt or know that others will remain guilty, we focus on the ego and this is another way to control lives. Love can heal the rifts caused by hurtful deeds. Forgiveness holds immense power because it mends separation. It moves us towards the unity and love that lies at the core of our being. It is a fundamental part of the healing process. We can also remember that at some time or another, we too have hurt someone through our own clumsy actions. These are times to learn from our past mistakes and do things differently. We need to be who we already are, love made in the image of God. If you don't love a person, you can't see them."

Intolerance or In Tolerance?

"I find that sometimes I am very intolerant of people," said Bill.

"The doorway of compassion is where you will develop forgiveness, compassion, and empathy and begin to celebrate the diversity and uniqueness inherent in all people. Compassion is defined as having an experience of "feeling-with" and deep empathy. Intolerance of differences always exists in people who don't know who they are; people who don't have a strong sense of their own authentic self, the soul within, or in short, intolerance is rooted in fear.

We talk about levels of consciousness. There is a group consciousness which is more of an ego consciousness. This is where we identify ourselves on the basis of the groups that we were born into or which side of the planet we come from. Then we move into the unity or the mystical consciousness where you honor your divinity. This means that we see that everyone is connected to everyone else. This means thinking more globally when we see all the divisions of different clothing or different skin.

Compassion is the joy of sharing, trying to understand the suffering of people, and being able to put ourselves in their shoes. It is not how much we give but how much love we put into the doing of the act-that is compassion in action. How we show love is to serve others and that means defining your higher purpose. Sometimes when we are attempting to walk a spiritual path to God life can also get harder as well as easier. I would like to tell you a story about Hal."

Do You Want A Friendship or a Fearship?

"I once had a good friend named Hal. Although we did not see each other often, when we finally got together we would talk, laugh, and simply enjoy each other. It did not really matter what we did because for us, being together was more important than having an agenda.

After about five years, something happened. We began to have ideas of how a friendship "should be". I even wrote a book about relationships called "The Book of Rules about Relationships". The trouble was that I had the only copy.

Our relationship changed from a state of being to one of doing. It changed from a verb which is a state of spontaneity and action, to a noun implying a "thing" which is still and dormant. It changed from feeling obliged to each other out of love to one of being an obligation, from expecting co-creatorship and joy in the relationship to an expectation, and from feeling responsible out of love for the other to a responsibility.

Sadly and not surprisingly, our friendship died. Gone was the unconditional love we once felt for each other and in its place was guilt, judgment, and disappointment for not meeting the others expectations. Our relationship changed from a friendship to a "fearship". It was easier for us to end the relationship than too look deeper into what was really going on. The effects were sad and devastating.

Each time we set up rules, conditions, and expectations that the other can most likely never fill, we feed the ego. The ego loves rules so that we can in some way think that we are insidiously controlling the other. This is one way that we can feel superior to another. Each time we put our obligations, responsibilities, and expectations on others, we setup guilt, judgment, and fear because we are afraid to not meet the conditions or requirements set forth in the friendship. We become very busy judging each other for not meeting the others expectations and become competitors keeping score of who did what to who, instead of co creators.

When we feed the ego, our identity and value come from outside and not inside us and we begin to demand performance in return for love. This is when we forget who we are in relationship to each other and begin to live in fear and disappointment of not being loved. We can't have a friendship with someone we fear, or we will be fearful within.

Often I see relationships deteriorate between parents and children, husbands and wives, and employers and employees. True friendships and relationships have no agenda and are not controlled by some set of conditions or rules set up from outside. True relationships are governed by love of the other, not expectations, obligations, and responsibilities. We all want to be loved for who we are and not what we do.

Fear, greed, and power come from the egos need to attach itself to something outside itself to obtain recognition and identity. It is important to develop our spiritual intelligence as well as our spiritual maturity for without this we will not have friendships but "fearships" in all our relationships. When we can access these deep dimensions of love, we can transcend our usual ways, defenses, identity, and beliefs about self and world. Here we trust that we are loved and that there is a sense of creativity and humility as well as an ability to access higher meanings in life."

Colleen: "*My mother is 93 years old and becoming feeble. I expect her to be like she was when I was young and perhaps she still expects me to be as I was as a child. Neither of us are the same but our love is still present. As soon as I set up my agenda and expectations, I can judge her and separate myself from her because it is too painful to see her dying. Perhaps now I can let go of my expectations of her and change them to ones of expectancy for times of joy; from feeling obligated to meet her expectations; to one of feeling obliged and thankful for our time left; and from one of seeing her as a responsibility and burden, to one of a choice of feeling responsible for her out of love. Then, we can truly enjoy our final moments on earth together*"

"When we put God in the center of our lives, we do not function by priorities but God weaves in and out of all our relationships, friends, family, work as a state of being and not doing. There is no control or agenda. We begin to respond to others from a state of love and trust, just like a child. Well yes, after all, I guess we are all children of God!"

The group all nodded.

Iye: "*God must have a big eraser to help us all.*"

"I doubt that God keeps score, but with that let's move on to the next door of love."

Chapter Fourteen

> *"The hunger for love is much more difficult to remove than the hunger for bread."*
>
> *-Mother Theresa-*

The Challenge of Door Four: Love

The Gift: Unconditional Love

"We are still in emotional intelligence and ready to enter the door of Love. Everyone looks very excited. Here we can release our fear of rejection, shine light on our understanding and learn to love ourselves unconditionally."

"How do you define love?" asked Iye.

"Love is difficult to define because love is silent and visual. Love takes place in the heart and often, we need to re-awaken the heart that has become closed. Weldwood, (1984) provides a framework for three principles of psychological and spiritual healing: (1) grounding; (2) letting go and (3) awakening the heart. Rowan (2007) speaks of a beautiful image of a person standing on the earth with arms outstretched to the open sky. The heart center is the balance point midway between these two points of the earth and sky. Our hearts must remain open for balance.

This is a photo given to me by a person who has worked very hard in many workshops to access his spiritual intelligence.

Without balance, our head is focused downward or in the clouds making it very hard to see when we walk. Weldwood describes this open hearted balance as being one of courage, humor, and compassion.

(Printed with the permission of Louis Rissland,2009)

Bishop Kallistos Ware, a theologian within the Greek Orthodox Church, writes: "The heart is open below to the abyss of the unconscious. It is open above to the abyss of Divine glory. The heart is the point of meeting between body and soul, between soul and spirit, between human freedom and Divine grace, between the comprehensible and the incomprehensible, between the created and the uncreated. It is the absolute center." (1997)

No Relationship, No Problem

"Despite our passion for romantic love, relationships are not the easiest way to find love and peace. They offer us a challenge. They are, however, one of the most effective ways for finding where we are blocked."

Iye:*"I was married three times said Iye and no matter who I married they always turned out to be someone else!"*

"It is in intimate relationships where we can see where we are not enlightened. Any relationship we have is a profound opportunity to recognize anything that would be unloving in you and gives you an opportunity to become more loving. The universe will always give you someone who will show you where you are judgmental or critical and every part that is not centered. Relationships naturally bring out into full view our desires, attachments, and unconscious programs, our likes, dislikes, belief systems, judgments, compulsions, conformities, etc. Relationships challenge us because they take us deep into thoughts, feelings, and experiences we have suppressed for a lifetime. That's why they provide the very best ground for personal growth!"

Mary:*" I am afraid that without a relationship, I will be lonely even though I am so unhappy in my marriage. I am afraid no one will want me. I know I want to end the marriage. I guess I am afraid of rejection".*

"Soul lives through relationships and it is in soul that we find meaning. We can have meaningful relationships with people, animals, groups, ideas, and ideals. We cannot force relationships however we can let love open the way to them.

No relationship, no problem; but also no growth. We can build a relationship with material things but they are things. Things cannot love us back. We can also have a relationship with an "idea" of a marriage and how it should be. Ideas cannot love us back. These are things are what will cause loneliness or alienation from life, or from your real self. Each relationship we have is an invitation to know God and the purpose of any relationship is to bring us closer to God. Ultimately, we have only one relationship and that is with God. Many of us can feel that we are spiritually evolved and at peace when we are by ourselves and later a relationship occurs and we begin to lose all sense of peace and feel like we are "going crazy." Separation from the soul or a sense of disconnection can leave you with an immense empty place, although you will seldom understand what that emptiness really is. What we really have is an unquenchable hunger for being reunited with our souls, for being made whole again. But that insatiable hunger almost always is experienced as a desire for something else: for a relationship, food, for numbing the pain, addictions, for excitement or other distractions from the pain, for material wealth and comfort, status and security, for a drink or a smoke or an orgasm, for more pleasure or less pain. It is our heart that makes us rich for we are rich according to who we are, not what we have."

Repairing the Broken Heart

Lisa: *"I feel like my heart as been broken. I gave my last boyfriend my heart. I am afraid to love again. So how can I repair my broken heart?"*

"Many of us who have had disappointing relationships feel like we gave our hearts away and that our hearts have been damaged. I believe that our biggest lesson is learning how to receive love again. We all know how to give. If we want to repair the damaged heart we need to let go of old patterns, beliefs, and roles in the here and now. An open heart only occurs in the present for it is only then that we are able to both give and receive love."

Lisa: *"Oh, that is how come we went through the door of forgiveness first?"*

"Yes. We want to move past forgiveness, defensiveness, and attack so that we can perform to our highest potential. Then we can tap into that greater spiritual identity and let the spiritual dimension take over so that our thoughts are God's thoughts and they become expressions of God's love. When we pass through door four, we can see the group process balances the grounding, letting go, and awakening of the heart. Love is a state of being and not doing. As we move through the fourth door, we move into that state of beingness. This is where we remember who we truly are."

Be. Do. Have.

Iye: *"Who am I?"*

"Before we know others, we must truly know ourselves. In the past, we have been defined by our relationships with others, how we have seen ourselves in relationship to others, how we think we have been treated by others, who we were told we were, should be and should not be. These were all sources that came from outside of us. Remember that you are not your beliefs. If you only see the faults in yourself and others, you will feed and strengthen the ego within yourself and that will get mirrored back."

"I had psychoanalysis for many years, said Bob, *and it never helped me."*

"Psychoanalysis does not work in helping us to know who we because it tells us *about* who we are. It's like we can know God or know *about* God. Who we are cannot be described in words but shown in moments of love. We attempt to live our lives backwards: we try to have more things, or more money, in order to do more of what we think we want so we will be happier. The way it actually works is the reverse. You must first be who you really are, then do what you love to do, in order to have what you want.

This quote on love comes from a Japanese therapist who believes that therapy is based on love, and that love is an important factor. It is love that makes the bridge between all the therapies. "The person I am, the 'I am this body, this mind, this chain of memories, this bundle of desires and fears' disappears, but something you may call identity, remains. It enables me to become a person when required. Love creates its own necessities, even of becoming a person." (Maharaj as cited in Almaas 1988, pp. 449 -50)

"It is important to learn to think of ourselves in terms of content and completeness within. Then we to begin to see the higher order of things, grasp the totality of who we are, understand how we arrived here. It is then that our higher purpose begins to become clear, and we begin to see the hidden harmony between ego and soul."

"Say more about love," said Iye.

"Love is an experience. The word experience is defined as (Langsheit): 1:an observation or participation in events, resulting in or tending toward knowledge, 2: knowledge, practice or skill derived from observation and participation in events: also: the length of such participation, 3: something encountered, undergone, or lived through, as by a person or community (1999). In the moments of truth, beauty and love we get glimpses of our soul or spirit. These are moments of being,"ing" words. These are moments where we can have altered states of consciousness and moments of feeling truly connected and at one with the universe. These are places of transcendence and moments of love. Maslow reported that peak experiences are the key to spiritual realms. He said that it is in peak experiences that people truly reach that state of being and obtain a sense of real self hood. (Maslow, 1962) These are the moments when we are completely and totally absorbed in the world. In Maslow's later books, he makes it clear that peak experiences are both examples of mystical experiences and examples of what the self is or could be. He describes how they gave meaning to his life and his writing. These peak experiences can be altered states of consciousness or places of transcendence where one feels one or in awe with the universe." (Rowan, 2007)

"I remember when my son was born, said Bob. *I never felt such a compete state of love, awe, and connection the very first time I held him."* The others nodded.

"Love is not something that can be defined in our rational intelligence. Love becomes part of our emotional intelligence when we take these peak experiences further and use them in relationship to other people and ourselves. Since love is an experience, let's look at what I call our moments of love. These are the moments that we use during Souldrama as an anchor to help us define our higher purpose. Remember that love is a state of Being and not Doing as opposed to the roles acted out in rational intelligence that we played to "get love". The Bible says that "God is Love" (1 John 4:8). Carl Jung said in an interview when he was asked if he believed in God he said "I could not say that I believe. I know. I have had the experience of being gripped by something stronger than myself, something that people call God." (1955)

Iye: *"Can you show me an example?"*

"Think of a time or visualize a scene in your life when you felt both loved and connected. This could be a glimpse or a remembrance of a scene in our lives with either people or animals or nature. I notice there are some tears here."

Mary: *" I want to begin my own health care agency but ever since my mother died two years ago, I feel paralyzed."*

"What was your moment of love Mary?"

"I remember once when I was small I had the flu and I was very sick. My mother who had 8 other children sat by my bed and rubbed my head and gave me water. She never left my side even when I was getting better."

"Let's look at that. Show us this moment Mary, and choose someone to be your mother. Invite her to come into this scene and show us what this scene looked like."

"I choose Maria to be my mother." (Mary sets up the scene with Maria)

"Now put yourself in the scene and experience this feeling. (Mary began to cry) Now choose someone to be you and to stand in your place."

"Colleen. Will you do this?"

"Colleen please take Mary's place and Mary please watch this moment as an observer. Tell me as you see this scene, what were you doing to feel loved and connected?"

"*Nothing,* she said sadly. *I was just lying there feeling my mother's love.*"

"Always remember that true love and connection are states of being and not doing. Lock this moment in your heart and remember you did not have to do anything to "get" it. You just had to be."

"*Maybe I can keep my mother's memory alive now by going forward to develop my own health care agency. Every time I help another person get well I will be keeping my mother's memory alive instead of being angry that she died. I will always remember this moment.*"

Colleen: "*I can't thank you enough Mary for choosing me and just giving me this moment of love. I never felt one with my own mother.*"

Doug : "*Thank you, Mary for helping me to remember her grandmother and how she would care for me by making special lunches and dinners when my mom was not home.*"

"What do you do now for a career Doug?"

"*I run a deli and luncheonette that is very successful and I love the work. Everyone says how special they feel here. I guess I can thank my grandmother. I have just begun to start an organization to feed the homeless.*"

Clare an artist: "*I remember walking in the woods with my brother, who died very young, and watching the sunset. Today my paintings of sunsets sell very quickly. I guess it is the love attached to the memory.*"

"Now you are getting the idea! I invite you all now to remember a moment of love from when you were young (if possible) and find the person in your original pair to share this memory. Let's have each of you now show the group in action what your memory was. Show how this sculpture is related to your higher purpose in life- your soul's mission! Put this memory into your heart.

Who was the Light Messenger you chose originally to help you, Mary?"

"*My Light Messenger was Love and I chose Maria to be the Light Messenger who could play the role of my Light Messenger, Love!*"

Maria: " *I always wanted children and it was wonderful to share that experience with you.*"

"Remember that in order to feel love and connected, we need to just be and not do. You helped us all to see this, Mary. Thank you."

Iye: *"Colleen and I both have the same moments when we got our first puppies. I really love taking photos of pets!"*

"Write down your moment of love and we will use this to move forward onto your higher purpose and see how you can transform that energy of love in your life. Now put this together with your spiritual gifts you received from your parents."

Iye: *"When I was young, my dog who I loved so much died and no one would tell me what happened to him-one day he was just gone."*

"Yes, that dog was your source of unconditional love and you were never allowed to say goodbye or have your feelings. It was there you learned not to trust. In this case, your parents would have dismissed your feelings as irrelevant and seen your grief as being a disturbance and a distraction from the familiarity of their own roles that they would have had to change if you felt your grief."

Iye: *"However, I love to take photos of people's pets so that they will always remember that unconditional love that existed between them. Perhaps this needed to happen so I could really learn to connect with my subjects from a distance. Come to think of it, I need to be good at distancing myself from the pets to catch them in their natural state. Something else to thank my mother for!"*

"Yes, that was a spiritual gift for your career, Iye. It will work well for your career in photography but not in relationships."

Colleen: *"I have been an accountant for 23 years and I really am unhappy. I realized today that I would rather be a veterinarian working with animals. I remembered with Iye's help, my very first puppy and how it gave me unconditional love in my chaotic family."*

"In this doorway, we made some of our moments of love conscious. The law of love is consciousness, and it is our consciousness that determines our relationships. Real communication is communion. This means that there is connection between the heart spaces between the two of you.

To sum these moments up: Therefore, when I say that 'I love,' it is not I who love, but in reality Love who acts through me. Love is not so much something I do as something that I am. Love is not a doing but a state of being - a relatedness, a connectedness to another mortal, an identification with her or him that simply flows within me and through me, independent of my intentions or my efforts."-- Robert A. Johnson (1999).

Unconditional Love

Maria: "*Sometimes, I feel judged by God and when things do not work out I feel as though I am being punished.*"

"If we feel judged by God, we often then are inclined to take the situation into our own hands to see how much better we can do than God. This feeds the ego."

Iye: "*So then we think we can become God. I have done that. Does God punish us for our actions?*"

"We punish ourselves. How can we be available to hear Gods messages if we hang onto our guilt? Sometimes, the only way we think to stay alive is to have some emotional drama where we think we are unworthy and God is punishing us. We spoke earlier about the roles we developed as children in doorway two when our soul's mission began to gain clarity and we began to see our parents as our spiritual teachers. As children, our parents are our higher power and therefore we think that love comes from something outside of ourselves. Often as we mature, our childish attitudes toward our higher power remain. Our relationship to God stays outside of ourselves as one being superficial and inconsistent. We continue to see God as one or both of our parents and this in turn tends to evoke a passive and helpless role in our relationship with God. If we know we have a loving God, then we will sincerely regret our actions and be willing to change our behavior and perceptions so that it does not happen again. (Miller,2000)

Bill nodded and said: "*I used to feel close to God only when a problem existed and I needed to ask for help or forgiveness. I felt that I must "do" something in order to have God's love, for I really did not feel as though I deserved it. I would bargain with him all the time.*"

"If we keep seeing God as something this is inconsistently outside of ourselves as opposed to within, then if we are not "rescued" by God, we begin to feel like a helpless victim and assume an aggressive or passive/aggressive stance which results in feelings of shame, guilt, abandonment, and further betrayal. Instead of moving forward, we engage in self-sabotaging behavior, compounding our problems." (Miller, 2000)

Bill: "*Then I would have a reason to drink more.*"

"Yes, your energy came from the problems in your life as opposed to the joy."

Iye: "*I am not so clear on all of this. I have a real problem loving myself.*"

"How do you see yourself as unlovable? Take a few minutes to write down the ways that you perceive yourself to be unlovable. Look at the list and see if you can identify where those characterizations originated. Can you pinpoint old messages from parents, teachers, and friends that led you to negative conclusions about yourself? Are those messages valid today?"

God is a Verb

"The beliefs we adopt as children usually don't hold when we view them objectively as adults. Can you let them go? Can you begin to see yourself as a unique expression of life, a genuine gift to the world?

Let's look at this. Choose someone in the room that could represent the role of your higher power or your God. Most of the hands are on your shoulder Iye and the second amount of hands are on Mary. I see that you chose Mary as well. Share with the person you chose, your reason for choosing them.

Iye, would you like to have a discussion with the God of your understanding?"

"Yes, I would like to choose Bill to play God."

Sitting Bill in God's chair Iye asks: *"God, how come I do not feel truly connected to you?"*

"Now Reverse roles Iye, with Bill and Bill please repeat back what Iye just said to you. Iye you are in the role of God." (Bill does so)

Iye answers from the role of God: *"I don't know. That's your problem,"*

"Iye and Bill please reverse roles again and Bill repeat back what Iye just told you to say as God (Bill does) Iye answers: *"What good are you! I have to do everything myself just as I have my whole life. You are exactly like my father, helpless."*

"Now Iye, come out of your seat and choose someone to be yourself. Stand by me and watch this interaction repeated." Iye chose Carlo to be himself.

The dialogue was repeated by Carlo as Iye watched the scene being replayed.

"What kind of God do you have Iye?"

"Helpless like my father."

"Is this how you want your God to be?"

"No."

"Iye, please sit in God's seat and let's have Bill sit over here (aside). Carlo remain in your seat in the role of Bill. Carlo please repeat the same question back to Iye now as he is in the role of the new God."

Carlo: *"How come I do not feel truly connected to you?"*

(To Iye as God) "Are you a loving God?"

"Yes."

"Then, respond as the God you desire to have, the mature, loving one. After a few minutes hesitation Iye said *"I always have a relationship with you, Iye, and I am always here for you. I love you more than you know. Simply ask for my help and it is done."*

"Now Iye, please reverse roles again with Carlo and Carlo would you please repeat this back to Iye using the words of his new mature loving God." Carlo answered as the New God.

Iye began to cry and said, *"I never realized my father was my God."*

"Iye this is your choice now, which God do you choose?"

Iye : *"The new, more loving God."*

"Can you now take your old God and put him into the hands of your new God?"

Iye does so and says: *"God can take care of you better than me. Go with God."*

"Good lets share now."

Carlo: *"I was so happy to be the new God as your drama showed me a more loving way to love myself."*

Bill: *"I was surprised you chose me Iye as your old God as my father was the same way. I could have taken your role easily and said the same thing. In fact I did! Thank you."*

"Let's share now in your original pairs and see if you can discuss some of the questions such as: How did you see God as a child? Now as an adult? What kind of relationship did you have and do you have now? How much has it matured?"

Clare: *"I was always taught to fear God. I can see it was not him but my father I feared."*

Iye: *"I always wondered how come I had a hard time "turning my life and will over to God" as requested in AA. Now I understand. Who would want a helpless God? So therefore, I had to become God. My new God is more loving than I could ever be and can never leave me. Truly then when I discover myself in another I can be delighted with that recognition and that is love."*

"What a beautiful way to put this! Jesus, a spiritual leader, taught that the entity that rules it is within man: "The kingdom of God is within you." He not only described this kingdom of the heavens in numerous parables but made its attainment by man the greatest object of human existence. In this doorway, love, we develop a sense of co-creator ship and feel called upon to serve and to give something back to the universe. We can do this through our moments of love and with the spiritual gifts we learned and earned from our parents in door two as we feel the gift of unconditional love for ourselves."

Carlo asked *"How does this fit with Moreno's theory and the action work we have done?"*

Good question. In the mid 1930's, when Moreno published his first book, psychology and spirituality were seen as different and separate. Yet, Moreno (1972), boldly suggested that individuals are co-creators with God, indicating self-responsibility in what one creates in life and in the world in general. God is not seen as a separate being, but rather as an expression of immanence - the indwelling of the Supreme Being. By this definition, all existence and each being is an expression of God. Theoretically, psychodrama is a holistic form of therapy addressing implicit, subconscious concepts of God. For Moreno (1972), part of living consciously is addressing individual views about God and spirituality. Moreover, Moreno (1972) saw spirituality as essential to clinical activities. In psychodrama, the protagonist can encounter God by using fellow participants to engage in spontaneous conversation and role reversal.(Miller, 2007). Taking on the role of a higher power, an individual will find oneself spontaneously coming up with individualized and surprisingly meaningful answers to that determine what kind of "relationship" that person has with their higher power. Is this higher power one that is critical, loving or punishing? Blatner (1998) defines spirituality as the activity of deepening our connectedness with the "Greater Wholeness of Being". He urged the need for creativity and imagery within the therapy process so humans can see themselves as co-creators and not victims of omnipotent strength. When God is seen as being inside and not outside of oneself, a greater sense of co-creative responsibility exists and the ability for a person to be authentic emerges, bringing the truth of the inner world of unconditional love to the outer world."

Bill: *"So God is inside of me and the more I love myself or God the more I will grow. Thank goodness! I think I got it!"*

Bernie Siegel said "I don't think God cares where we were graduated or what we did for a living. God wants to know who we are. Discovering this is the work of the soul. It is our true life's work." "We were created to be loved and that happens in relationship. When we act as though we were created to be unloved, then we limit ourselves. God is a state of being and is a verb. A verb takes action and does not stay stagnant for when it does, it dies. Decide first what you want to be and take action to do what you have to do."

Iye: *"Thanks to the group and the action work, I am really beginning to feel self love."*

"The Buddha said it well.""You, yourself, as much as anybody in the entire universe, deserve your love and affection."

"When you can lead a life expressing this belief, your mind and heart begin to open to new realities, and other dimensional truths become known. Now we are ready to move onto the next level of spiritual intelligence. In order for us to get to this level, we had to gather the gifts of trust, clarity, forgiveness, and unconditional self love. Everyone has worked very hard. We will be taking a break for a day and resting so we can take some time to integrate all we have learned and have some fun. I will see you all the day after tomorrow."

When you are aware that you are the force that is Life, anything is possible. Miracles happen all the time, because those miracles are performed by the heart. The heart is in direct communion with the human soul, and when the heart speaks, even with the resistance of the head, something inside you changes; your heart opens another heart, and true love is possible." - Don Miguel Ruiz

Chapter Fifteen

The Land of Spiritual Intelligence

Feeding the Soul

"So we have had a day off to relax and I congratulate you all! It is time to give yourselves a round of applause for your great work! We have now bridged the gap, moved over to our right brain, and are ready reconnect to our spiritual intelligence. Our rational and emotional intelligences are in balance. Iye you seem quite excited, what is it?"

"I had a chance to visit this land of SQ. The land here is green and full of flowers. The colors are amazing and the aromas are just as wonderful. It is like it is spring here! Everything seems so alive and vibrant. The colors have an energy of their own. The people here are kind and welcoming and laugh often. They seem to have few fears and worries and live in the present. People notice the clouds and the flowers! They even have gardens here ready to harvest!

I met a girl. Her name is Skylar and her name means "eternal life, strength, love and beauty." She likes to be called Skye for short. Skye does not live in the past but stays ever present in the moment. I asked her if she ever worried about finding a partner and she looked at me and said she trusted that the perfect person would soon appear. Skye dedicates her life to the poor teaching and helping them to express themselves through art and pottery. Her purpose is her relationship with her work and with everything around her. Skye never asks "why?", only how, when, where, who and what. She accepts and co-creates. She has done much personal growth and healing in the past so that she could develop a healthy relationship with herself and

God. I feel like I have known her all my life! Maybe she is a part of me that I have forgotten. Thank you for bringing us here."

"It could very well be that she is a part of you that you have forgotten. By looking at the group, I can tell that everyone is very happy for you! Skye can most likely integrate many inputs at once and do intuitive and holistic thinking. Remember how we said back in the land of ego, that the girl of your dreams is probably an artist, craftswoman, or musician? The right brain hemisphere is the part of the brain that controls our spiritual intelligence or SQ in the land of Soul where Skye resides and where we have arrived now. We are now on the side of the brain that is the seat of passion and dreams.

You can see by looking at this land that the gardens have been planted and the seeds have been randomly sown by the wind to grow where they may. The outcome is a burst of natural beauty. No one here tries to control the outcome. Here there is no separation and everything is one."

"I feel so great I am not going to even ask you to define spiritual intelligence! I am looking around and it is so wonderful to have the group share my joy! Skye said she is very happy that she met me and remembers living once in the state of Ego".

"I am very happy for you and now as your ego has become thinner, let's not forget to recognize and honor it by talking a bit more about SQ, for in this land the ego is honored as it has aligned with the soul."

Soul Skills

"As we reach this stage of SQ, we are able to believe in ourselves, our purpose, and be vision and be value led, acting from beliefs, principles and self love. We have developed spiritual maturity. "First, consider that many if not most people do not go on beyond ordinary maturity. You need to actually have some idea of what you're working on and get on with it. If ordinary maturity involves the development of what I might call "ego skills," external life management skills, then deep maturity involves "soul skills," working on finishing up the many types of unfinished business in your psychological self. It might include such elements as deepening your sense of belonging-ness, connected-ness, philosophy of life, working out personal issues, developing a degree of wisdom, and the like " (Blatner, 2000).

Maria: *"So we have accumulated the gifts of the doorways of Trust, Clarity, Forgiveness, and Unconditional Love. Did we need to accumulate all these qualities before we could enter the land of spiritual intelligence?"*

"Yes. We have entered four doorways; the first was faith and the gift was trust. As we prepare our own gardens, we must first trust and grow in loving those around us with understanding and compassion. When we are free to do this, we can love and trust without an agenda and expectations. It is here that we can see the God within each of us and begin to feel the ego give up some control as we surrender and have faith.

When we entered the door of truth, we found that we could find the grace to make sense of some of the tragedies in our lives – we could let go of the suffering from the old wounds of our past and find the grace to make sense of these wounds for our higher purpose. We realized that grace does not depend on suffering to exist but where there is suffering we can find grace.

When we entered the third door of compassion, we were rewarded with the gift of forgiveness. It was there that we could let go of our judgments and guilt of self and others. We realized that the guilt we felt helped us to conform to outside ethics and not to our inner voices. It was here that we learned the truth; we were putting off dealing with the truth of our emotions. Our mistakes helped us to grow so that we can now more clearly see our life's purpose. Our egos began to get thinner."

Bob: *"I feel so much more love."*

"You were always loved – the love inside you did not grow, but simply expanded as your ego became thinner to align with the soul. When we found unconditional love in door four, it was in the knowing a unconditional loving higher power that helped our love to expand and grow. We no longer knew **about** God but we came to **know** an unconditional and all loving God, a God of being and not doing. We would be blind to the beauty in this land of Spiritual Intelligence until we were able to open our hearts to receive this love.

If cognitive intelligence is about thinking and emotional intelligence is about feeling, then spiritual intelligence is about being. In a holistic view of life, we are creatures with a mind, a body, and a spirit—all interconnected and arranged in a pattern that means that the whole is greater than the sum of the parts. In the same way, we can look at our intelligences. (Miller, 2007)

We have discussed rational and emotional intelligences. Now, there exists much scientific data that points to the presence of a spiritual intelligence (SQ), the ultimate intelligence that serves as a necessary foundation for the effective functioning of both IQ and EQ cite some of those sources. The category of skills that is crucial for wholeness, happiness, and effective living, I call Spiritual Intelligence (Miller, 2007). Spiritual Intelligence refers to the skills, abilities and behaviors we need to help us balance the expansive love that flows through our hearts and all of creation with the need for discipline and responsibility. When we successfully balance these polarities in our own feelings and in how we treat others and the world, we are able to create forgiveness, healing and connection and in fact we are co-creating with God.

Spiritual intelligence is inherently difficult to define. It is quite separate from organized religion. SQ is about questions more than answers. It lives in stories, poetry and metaphors, as well as uncertainty and paradox. The word 'religion' comes from roots which mean to 'tie together,' that the spiritual involves not only faith which is vision, a way of seeing and a way of doing life with prayer and values, but also obligations to and support from others (Miller, 2007) . One way of conceptualizing spiritual intelligence is offered by Adams (1995) as a devotion to discovering, exploring, and living in accordance with the depth dimensions of existence. The depth dimensions are ways of being that transcend our usual ways, defenses, identity, and beliefs about self and world. Here, we trust that we are loved and that there is a sense of creativity and humility and an ability to access higher meanings in life."

Bob: *"So if I become spiritually intelligent I will become poor?"*

Money Talks But it Can't Love You Back

"Not at all. Money can be a very spiritual concept helping us to live a spiritual life with purpose and values. However, money is one of today's top stressors and many people are seeking counseling for financial problems. They seem to suffer from a deep lack of self-esteem related to money. Their problems come not from money itself, but from their deepest fears, fantasies, and their relationship with money. What remains unconscious can control our behavior. Unless we face our hidden beliefs and fears about money and make them conscious, we will sabotage our relationships as well as our sense of self."

Bob: *"I grew up in a very wealthy family. I never felt really loved."*

"Recently, I watched a program about children of billionaires. It is now evident that not only financially poor people are having problems today but so are the wealthy who have become what I call "spiritually poor". These children of wealth never developed a sense of connection and belonging and later in their lives often have difficulty experiencing true intimacy. They had all the money and material things they ever would need, but money, like things cannot love us back.

Few of these children were allowed to go to the park and choose their playmates When they did , they were forbidden to invite these children into their homes, or if they did, the families of the neighborhood children would judge them for having "more " than they did and stop them from playing together. Eventually, they had to choose their friends from a select, exclusive group of other children of wealth. They missed opportunities to interact and develop relationships with diverse cultures. These children began to feel isolated, lonely, and different than their peers. Later, would money become the substitute for their self-esteem and give them a sense of connection and belonging? Would it become their Higher Power? Would money love them back?"

Bob: *"I would have loved to have my father just toss the ball with me."*

"Yes, Bob. What these children craved was time with their parents. Time was a commodity that was not available to them while both parents were unavailable working to maintain their money and status. Few of these children were lucky enough to have a consistent nanny that brought them up. Many of them had maids and a series of nannies. They learned that people could be hired to care for them and that money could temporality buy "love". They also learned that someone had to be "paid" to love and care for them, and since they were nothing but employees, they could be dismissed at anytime. They also learned that relationships were inconstant and not to be trusted. Later, how much time and energy would they want to invest in intimacy? Intimacy means "into- me- see." Who really saw these children? How did they learn self-esteem? What they did learn was that it was easier to count on money than people.

They learned to respond to authority with money. How does one develop a tolerance to frustration when money can take care of all their problems? What happens to these children later when it comes time to discover their own dreams? Are they even allowed to have their own dreams after getting whatever they wanted in life? Did they feel obliged to remain in the family business?

Iye: *"I am afraid to leave the family to go and have my own dream."*

"So it is necessary to look at our fears, including the fear of failure. Is the unspoken message "You will be thrown out of the family if you become successful? When you have experienced he loneliness, lack of love, and connection that having wealth brings, you may never want to continue in the family business. Then what happens? If you decide to follow your own dreams, will you be as successful as your parents? The fear of abandonment is so great in an isolated family that often we do nothing to follow our own dreams. Perhaps it would be safer and easier to inherit the built in success rather than deal with the fear of failure."

"This sounds exactly right."

"Will money fill that empty hole inside of us? What is the attachment to things outside of us for love and security? Maybe it is not the money that is the problem but our relationship to money. Like anything that we attach to outside of ourselves, food, drugs, or alcohol, we look for it to give us temporary relief; a quick fix, and great mood swings. And, like anything in our lives we can build a tolerance to things that come from outside of ourselves, which results in wanting more. We become so busy "getting" something that we lose our sense of being."

Iye: *"Perhaps the Beatles were right "Money Can't Buy Me Love"*

Self Worth or Net Worth?

"Do we judge our own value by how much money we have? Can we put a value on self worth? Henry Ward Beecher said "No one can tell whether they are richer or poorer by turning to their ledger. It is the heart that makes a person rich. One is rich according to what one is, not according to what one has."

"Never having an identity, can money give us one? Do we mortgage our souls for false security? Let's look at some of our beliefs and attitudes about money including the "no talk" rules that exist in our families. Often, just talking about money brings about much anxiety and secrecy. Most people will talk about sex before they talk about money. Money is the thing most often lied about in marriages and relationships. Are we told not to talk about money in a household even though our material wealth or lack of it is visible? What are those fears and unlived dreams that are that are hidden, unspoken and secret in your family? What are the rules and roles about money that you learned?"

Colleen: *"There was much shame in my family for not having money. At least it was talked about but my mother always compared us to families that had so much more."*

Bill: *"I was judged by where I lived. My mother thought that having money would make us look perfect while it only made me feel disconnected."*

Iye: *"I always thought that if I became poor, I would be seen as lesser than, or as an outcast, lazy, oppressed, foolish, and undesirable".*

Lisa: *"My family thought that money was the root of all evil."*

Carlo: *"In my family we thought that people with money signified superiority, happiness, belonging, wisdom, sex appeal, perfection and even spiritual superiority."*

"What are your cultural beliefs about money? Are people with money more deserving? Do we think that people with money have no problems? Money has many emotional uses: power, withholding love, gaining a sense of belonging and connection, a mood manager, keeping score, obtaining self worth, freedom, and identity.

Are these some of the beliefs you hold today? "There will never be enough; never tell anyone how much money you have. Are these beliefs internalized so that we may have a false sense of victimization or helplessness? I am entitled to all I can get because look at all I suffered.

Fill in the blank......Money is_____.When was the first time you even realized that there was such a thing as money? How do you use money to enhance your connections with friends and family? Remember, the ego loves to define itself by things outside of itself. You are not your money. What is the spiritual meaning of money?"

Spiritual Capitol

"We can have money intelligence but what about a spiritual intelligence? Maybe it is time to build spiritual capitol instead of material capitol. Similar to the game of Monopoly, we spend our lives trying to "get" more to "be" more, sacrificing and mortgaging our souls to be loved. In the end, though, like the game, everything we worked for all goes back in the box and all that is left is love; the very thing for which we have been searching. Fear, doubt, anxiety, and disbelief all serve to repel abundance from us. Faith, love, and gratitude for the gifts of our lives keep energy and abundance flowing. The more we trust in our well being, the more it will be realized.

We need to develop our spiritual intelligence so that we can gain spiritual capitol in our world and therefore build financial recovery. We can build spiritual capitol with our spiritual intelligence. The concept of Spiritual capitol can establish a base on which there is mutual trust and communication in organizations. Spiritual capital reflects the core values, the person's value systems and the internal driving force of human beings and these qualities are essential to build lasting relationships among people of different backgrounds. It addresses those concerns about what it means to be human and the ultimate meaning and purpose of human life

Zohar (2005), reports that spiritual intelligence is badly needed in our market economies today. It allows people of different backgrounds to understand each other in friendly terms, to think creatively, and change the rules and their roles in their lives according to new situations. It allows people to think about all kinds of possibilities and vision in life. When we develop our spiritual intelligence, we have the ability to dissolve old ways of thinking that puts too much emphasis on material capital.

Spiritual intelligence is a way of thinking using the peace of God within. Spiritual intelligence does not mean being clever for that implies short-sightedness and this is different from true spiritual wisdom. Many politicians are clever in order to attain an outside goal and are motivated by self interest –the gains are short sighted. Spiritual intelligence sees the larger whole and how we are all connected. Just as cleverness divides feeding the ego saying, "I am better than you", spiritual intelligence includes and unites."

"Are there any ways to help us focus on what factors are necessary for spiritual intelligence? asked Bob?"

In 1999, Gardner reported seven factors that are necessary for spiritual intelligence and behavior:

- divinity, the sense of connection to a God figure or Divine Energy Source;

- mindfulness, an awareness of the interconnection of the mind and body, with an emphasis on practices that enhance that relationship;

- intellectuality, a cognitive and inquiring approach to spirituality, with a focus on understanding sacred texts;

- community, the quality of spirituality connecting to the community at large;

- extrasensory perception, spiritual feelings, and perceptions associated with non rational ways of knowing;
- childhood spirituality, a personal, historical association to spirituality through family tradition and activity;
- trauma, a stimulus to spiritual awareness through experiencing physical or emotional illness or trauma to the self or a loved one.

Some of the qualities of Spiritual Intelligence are values such as courage, integrity, intuition, and compassion and love. These imply responsibility to one another. Developing our spiritual intelligence is critical today so that we can have a strong enough inner world to sustain on our need for belonging, self- esteem, contribution, and love. When we develop our spiritual intelligence, we can begin to ask ourselves why we are doing what we are doing and then seek some fundamentally better way of doing it. As human beings, we live by meaning and purpose, not by status or pleasure. Maybe having less will make us depend on others more and to rely on our inner resources.

Elizabeth Dunn (2008) from the University of British Columbia did a study that showed that spending five dollars on someone else a promoted greater sense of happiness and connection than buying something for yourself. When we are busy trying to "get" more, to be more, then we avoid the very things that would make us happier such as donating to charities or spending time with others."

Bill: *"How does Spiritual intelligence relate to my career?"*

"For many of us, work is a means to an end--to acquire possessions, maintain our sense of identity, and improve our lifestyle. For some people, however, work can also be a means of avoiding distress through channeling their energies into relationships, or addictions. Our work can be an expression of who we are or it can be a job. We can make a living or a dying. Finding our purpose and expressing our gifts can be a life long journey. Rather than referring to a "career," we may need to reflect about the meaning of our work at various stages in our lives. More commonly today, it takes a few turns and changes of direction for us to find us fulfillment in life. Building your SQ may help you when you reassess your work situation. For different reasons, many people around the world are unhappy and this can be an opportunity to look at work as a possible area of change.

Deepak Chopra (2000) said "There are many aspects to success; material wealth is only one component. .But success also includes good health, energy and enthusiasm for life, fulfilling relationships, creative freedom, emotional and psychological stability, a sense of well-being, and peace of mind." Zohar has written a great deal about the types of intelligence that correlate to the three types of capital those truly great spiritual leaders must integrate: material, social, and spiritual. Zohar, (2005) states that great leadership depends primarily on vision that we can appreciate intellectually, emotionally, and spiritually. She goes further and states that vision is the passion and driving force of our enterprise. What appear to be lacking today are leaders without vision. We all have a vision and purpose. Remember how easy it was to make your vision boards."

"One reason that visionary leadership is in short supply today is the value our society places on one particular kind of capital--material capital. Too often, the worth or value of an enterprise is judged by how much money it earns at the end of the day, or how much worldly power it gives us over others. This obsession with material gain has led to short-term thinking and the narrow pursuit of self-interest. It is true that any kind of enterprise we want to engage in requires some kind of financial wealth if it is to succeed in the short-term. But for leadership to inspire long-term, sustainable enterprises, it needs to pursue two other forms of capital as well: social and spiritual. These three types of capital resemble the layers in a wedding cake. Material capital is the top layer, social capital lies in the middle, and spiritual capital rests on the bottom, supporting all three. IQ, or intelligence quotient, was discovered in the early 20th century and is tested using the Stanford-Binet Intelligence scales. It refers to our rational, logical, rule-bound, problem-solving intelligence. It is supposed to make us bright or dim. It is also a style of rational, goal-oriented thinking. All of us use some IQ, or we wouldn't be functional.

SQ, our spiritual intelligence quotient, underpins IQ and EQ. Spiritual intelligence is ability to access higher meanings, values, abiding purposes, and unconscious aspects of the self and to embed these meanings, values, and purposes in living a richer and more creative life. Signs of high SQ include an ability to think out of the box, humility, and an access to energies that come from something beyond the ego, beyond just me and my day-to-day concerns. SQ is the ultimate intelligence of the visionary leader. It was the intelligence that guided men and women like Churchill, Gandhi, Nelson Mandela, Martin Luther King Jr., and Mother Teresa. The secret of their

leadership was their ability to inspire people, to give them a sense of
something worth struggling for."

Iye: *"Can we store up spiritual intelligence?"*

"We have no need to when we live in the present free from fear
and worry. We cannot store up spontaneity. Think about laughter-can
that be stored? We can store up anxiety and fear if we are constantly
worrying about the future and not trusting. This will feed the ego."

Iye: *"How does Spiritual Intelligences apply to work and*
corporations? What do we need to become spiritual leaders?"

"There are twelve necessary components (Zohar, 2005)
recognizes for spiritually intelligent leadership. These are the
components that are woven into the action stages of Souldrama. While
they overlap into each stage of development, they serve a primary
function in each stage.

1. *Self-Awareness*: Knowing what I believe in and value,
   and what deeply motivates me.

2. *Spontaneity*: Living in and being responsive to the
   moment.

3. *Being Vision- and Value-Led*: Acting from principles
   and deep beliefs, and living accordingly.

4. *Holism*: Seeing larger patterns, relationships, and
   connections; having a sense of belonging.

5. *Compassion*: Having the quality of "feeling-with" and
   deep empathy.

6. *Celebration of Diversity:* Valuing other people for their
   differences, not despite them.

7. *Field Independence*: Standing against the crowd and
   having one's own convictions.

8. *Humility*: Having the sense of being a player in a larger
   drama, of one's true place in the world.

9. *Tendency to Ask Fundamental "Why?" Questions*:
   Needing to understand things and get to the bottom of
   them.

10. *10. Ability to Reframe*: Standing back from a situation
    or problem and seeing the bigger picture; seeing
    problems in a wider context.

11.   *11. Positive Use of Adversity*: Learning and growing from mistakes, setbacks, and suffering.
12.   *12. Sense of Vocation*: Feeling called upon to serve, to give something back."

"How can I become more spiritually intelligent in my relationships?" asked Mary.

"Some of the qualities of SQ are values such as courage, integrity, intuition, and compassion and love. These imply responsibility to one another. With SQ, more is less; as you learn, the process may involve unlearning what other people have taught you. Spirituality is an essential component of a holistic approach to life and work. It finds expression in creativity and all forms of the arts. The more aware you become, you let go of your old roles and the ego is reduced by removing all thoughts of "I" and "mine." This gradual process of reduction calms the mind further and leads to the experiencing of progressively deeper levels of peace and happiness.

Lately, I have been traveling throughout the world doing workshops, teaching, and training a group experiential method how of how access our spiritual intelligence. I have seen many types of money. I have seen many things written on various currencies. So far, I have never seen *"In Money We Trust"* written on any of them. "In God We Trust." is written on our money. This says it all. Yes, money talks; but maybe we are not really listening."

> *"The intuitive mind is a sacred gift and the rational mind is a faithful servant. We have created a society that honours the servant and has forgotten the gift."*
>
> *–Einstein-*

Chapter Sixteen

> *"The sufficiency of my merit is to know that my merit is not sufficient."*
>
> *-St.Augustine -*

The Challenge of Door Five: Humility

The Gift: Empowerment

"As we begin our journey into the land of spiritual intelligence, we are now ready to enter into fifth door of humility. This is where we ask to be guided toward our vision so that we may find freedom in our principles, innocence in our values, and trust in the awakening of our personal power. In order to make a difference and know that our life has been worthwhile, we must operate from a higher level of consciousness –our spiritual intelligence-the land in which our soul dwells. St. Augustine said: "Do you wish to be great? Then begin by being. Do you desire to construct a vast and lofty fabric? Think first about the foundations of humility. The higher your structure is to be, the deeper must be its foundation."

Bill: *"What does humility mean?"*

"Humility, as we use it here, means having a sense of being a player in a larger drama and in having a sense of one's true place in the world."

Carlo: *"Oh, like being a player on a sports team."*

"Yes, humility or being humble is what defines an unpretentious and modest person. Someone who does not think that he or she is better or more important that the others. The opposite of humility is pride. The concept of humility addresses intrinsic self-worth and is often emphasized in the realm of religious and ethical practices."

Iye: *"Sometimes it is hard to be a spiritual person and really stand firm in my beliefs. I have a lot of questions. How does the new me, the more whole me, fit in the wider world? What is my purpose, where and how do I belong in the universe? How does my purpose fit with my greater sense of what it is all about? Will I have the courage to stand up for my beliefs? People at home laugh at me when I tell them I want to move and leave my career as a scientist and open a photography shop. They tell me I will never make it and they tell me that I should stay with a secure job."*

"Part of the lesson in doorway five is learning to have the courage to stand against the crowd and have your own convictions. It is hard to be yourself in a world that is constantly trying to have you be someone else. Now you will be able to be able to build upon all the lessons you have learned and you will be able to turn within to look for the answers."

Iye: *"How do I know when I am not being true to myself?"*

"All blocks arise when we are not being authentic, when we are not being true to ourselves. We know we are not being authentic when we feel discomfort of any kind. Always trust that your soul knows what is best for you. Believe in yourself and act on your ideas. Give yourself permission to do what you want with your life. As you know yourself, you will know your own power."

Iye: *"I have seen so much happen here within the group this week. This has really restored my faith in God, others and within myself. I can see my vision actually happen. In fact, I can envision my own studio and actually myself teaching photography to others."*

"We spend time blaming others or finding excuses for things not being what we want them to be, and not enough energy putting ourselves on the line growing out of the past, taking risks, and getting on with our lives. True spiritual intelligence means we stop blaming others for who did what and trust that there is a higher force deep within that will never leave us."

Bob: *"Sometimes I think I am too stupid to do things or that I am not smart enough."*

"The truth is that we already have everything we need to be on our higher purpose. We are all given these abilities through our parents and divine creator. It is through these gifts that we have the ability to be able to do anything that sparks our creativity and passion. Our abilities cannot be measured on an IQ test. If you can believe this about yourself, you will never think "I'm too stupid" again. Creativity and intuition are meaningless unless you put the ideas that arise into action. We must make some effort to do things differently or to do different things, or our lives remain the same.

Remember talking about Moreno? (1972) He believed that creativity is best evoked via spontaneous improvisation rather than planned rational behavior. For Moreno, to be spontaneous was to connect with one's inner core, searching within to find answers to struggles rather than seeking direction from other people. Victor Frankl proposed including the spiritual into psychology, that is, into the psychology of the unconscious. (1972) He referred to the struggle to have the courage to just be, and to live life authentically. "We had to learn ourselves, and furthermore we had to teach the despairing men, that it did not matter what we expected from life, but rather what life expected from us. We needed to stop asking about the meaning of life but instead to think of ourselves as those who were being questioned by life, daily and hourly. Our answer must consist not in talk and medication, but in right action and in right conduct. Life ultimately means taking the responsibility to find the right answer to its problems and to fulfill the tasks which it constantly sets for the individual."

When we view God as being within, constantly inviting creativity, we are challenged to live each moment consciously and with vitality. This implies a belief that we have free will, self determinism, and are capable of solving our own problems. Moreover, it suggests a capacity to recreate ourselves. In this way, our existence is never fixed but in a constant state of transition; we are constantly emerging and becoming. Moreno promoted a mindset of engaging in creative life experiences to find meaning, significance, and purpose."

Maria: *"I have felt so accepted here even when expressing individual ideas which may not conform to the rest of the group. What I have learned is that I can belong to the group without being forced to suppress my feelings or ideas. I feel loved within this group."*

"One of the benefits of the method of psychodrama is that it allows for self-expression, whether unconventional or traditional. For this reason individuality is encouraged over allegiance to group norms (Blatner, 2000). Yalom (1975) suggested that participation in a group allows for members to learn how to learn the development of socializing techniques, resolve conflicts, to be helpful, to be less judgmental, and to be more empathic. By using psychodrama as a therapeutic method in Souldrama, you have developed these skills and learned to relate to others in the group in a healthy way through intense experiential events. This has been a powerful modality for learning, as you can take the skills that you have learned in all the previous doorways and us them outside the group experience."

Iye: *"So in this doorway of humility, I really have really become aware of what I believe in and value, and what deeply motivates me.*

And I had lost the ability to appreciate the positives in life and, more importantly, I had lost a commitment to take action, or to make a difference in this world."

Mary: *"When my child had cancer, she would never think about how sick she was, she would only imagine herself playing with her friends and swimming in the summer. She got better and I believe a lot of her healing had to do with the vision she had of herself being well again."*

"Children seem to do this naturally as they use all parts of their brain. In the Bible it says "As you think, so shall you be." Most of our obstacles would melt away if, instead we just took action and moved forward. Let's look at your vision board you did in doorway two, Iye.

Now, Choose different people to represent different parts of your board; give them a message to repeat to you. Now let's stand back and see your board in action.

(Iye chooses people to represent parts of his board and gives them a message.) I would like you to all say your messages to Iye and move into action."

"Wow! This is a vision of my life and how beautiful it is! Look at the woman I put on the board a few days ago-she looks just like Skye and I did not even know her. Here is the picture of my photography studio. Here are all the other things that I put up there not even knowing what I wanted; a picture of me with my photography studio, me teaching, a home in the mountains overlooking the ocean, a picture of a woman who looked like Skye helping children, beautiful scenery in the mountains. How did this happen? Thank you all!'

"I guess your soul knows what it wants! It is important to visualize yourself as though you have already arrived. Similar to Moreno's (1971) psychodrama the experiential component of bringing the unconscious into consciousness, concretizing it and acting it out allows for an awareness and clarity difficult to come by other therapeutic means. Active imagination and psychodrama are both experiential, spontaneous and undirected methods designed to express the thoughts and wishes of the ego. Jung (1957) found the experiential nature of active imagination to be central to healing the soul. Active imagination seems to support Moreno's (1971) view that wholeness is a result of bringing the unconscious into conscious awareness. The psyche is considered by both Jung (1957) and Moreno (1971) to be an observable fact. Similar to psychodrama, active imagination is a way to directly experience our inner life while still maintaining our conscious sense of self as observer (Jung, 1957). Jung (1957) believed active imagination to be a spontaneous, experiential process that allows unconscious images to be revealed with little conscious intervention.. Jung (1957) would direct his clients to clear their mind so that an image could arise. After a moment of directed concentration images would spontaneously appear. Clients would then be encouraged to verbally and physically act them out, entering the scene and becoming a part of the action, directly experiencing their unconscious images. Jung (1957) believed that rather than verbally processing or cognitively reviewing psychic material, the physical experiencing of the unconscious offers a transforming experience. Thus, one is able to transcend and heal division of the ego."

Iye: *"This board is a beautiful vision of my life to come and so is everyone else's."*

"The doorway to self-empowerment opens when we become Vision and Value Led and we act from principles, deep beliefs, and live accordingly. Now let's look at each other's boards and stand by the one you are attracted to. Share what attracts you to this board. Is this board most like yours or do they have something on theirs that you may have forgotten?"

Mary: *"This reminds me of what Oriah Mountain Dreamer said "It doesn't interest me what you do for a living. ...I want to know what you ache for, and if you dare to dream of meeting your heart's longing."*

"Yes, this is beautiful. Before we move onto the next doorway of gratitude, I would like you to listen to a very beautiful story a friend of mine, TT Srinath (2009) wrote. This is a wonderful ending to this doorway where the gift is self-empowerment and a beautiful introduction to the next doorway of gratitude."

"Life is simple and requests of us submission with joy. Submission comes unhesitatingly to each of us when we live with respect, chiefly for ourselves, gratitude, and humility.

A passenger rushing to board his train at a railway station noticed a beggar seated on the platform with a cloth spread before him. Seeing some pencils lying on the cloth, he stopped briefly and asked the beggar if the pencils were for sale. The beggar looked up and said 'yes'. The passenger quickly dropped a couple of rupees on the cloth, picked up the pencils and left. Many years later, the man was at a party when a well-dressed, middle aged man came up to him and said, "Sir, do you remember me?" But the man couldn't place him and thought he might be a successful businessman who wished to engage in conversation. The stranger then saluted him and said, "I am indebted to you, sir, for having restored in me my self-respect." Surprised, the man asked the stranger who he was and what he had done for him. "Many years ago you bought pencils from me on a railway platform and gave me back my lost faith in myself. Thank you," the stranger replied.

Self-respect is one of the most powerful ingredients for restoring pride in oneself and living a full life. When we respect ourselves, we begin to discover who we are. We awake to everything, and recognise that everyone and everything are equally precious and whole and good. We discover what is confused in us and what is brilliant, what is bitter and what is sweet. In effect, it is not just ourselves that we discover but also the universe.

When I respect myself I respect others, for what I do not do for myself I cannot do for others. When I love myself I learn to love others. When I appreciate myself I learn to appreciate others. When I allow myself to be happy and enjoy every moment of my existence I encourage others also to do so. I become compassionate, accepting, and non-judgmental of myself and those whom I receive into my life. One feels confident and fearless about looking into someone else's eyes.

Gratitude is the singular quality that allows me to live in abundance.

A child once asked his rich father to take him to visit a slum. When they got there, they went towards the hut of a potter. The child noticed a little stream of water running into an open drain and several children and dogs playing outside the hut, which was illuminated by a kerosene lamp. Going around the hut, they saw a vast dump with children and dogs playing on it.

The child was satisfied and asked the father to take him home. The father was curious to know what the child had understood of this experience. The child looked dolefully at his father and said, "Thank you, father, for showing me how poor we are and how rich the potter is." The father became confused. The child went on to explain, "I am grateful that I have seen so much of abundance in the potter's life that I do not see in ours. We have electric lights, so limited in glow, to brighten our homes while the potter has the whole sky, the moon and shining stars to lighten his existence. We have a little pond at the back of our house; the potter has a small river running in front of his hut.

We have only one pet and the potter has so many dogs to play with. Few children visit our house while the potter has several children playing in his house. We have no backyard and the potter has a whole dump. I am glad I am able to recognise the poverty of our life."

True gratitude comes from recognizing the preciousness and bounty of life's offering. Each morning when I wake up, I sit down and write a page of gratitude. I acknowledge all that I am being offered as a gift and celebrate each offering with thankfulness. I am able to accept without demand and, most important, to be able to live in wonderment.

Humility comes when I offer myself in the moment with contentment and devotion. I recognize my awakened heart as I no longer shield my vulnerability from the fragility of my existence.

I neither grasp nor reject but enter into a relationship valuing myself and valuing the other. I neither defend nor do I have the need to prove.

The Arya Samaj movement in Bengal was gaining immense popularity during the lifetime of the sage Ramakrishna Paramahamsa. The Samajis believed that knowledge or gnana, rather than devotion or bhakthi, was more important to achieve moksha or salvation. Ramakrishna Paramahamsa personified bhakthi and the Samajis decided to engage him in a discussion to prove he was poorly schooled in the Vedas. On the appointed day, a senior member of the Samaj reached Ramakrishna's humble abode and invited him to a debate. Ramakrishna unhesitatingly bowed before the wise man and requested him to ask his questions. The erudite Samaji held forth on the benefits of the Upanishads and asked Ramakrishna several questions. To each question, Ramakrishna bowed low and acknowledged his ignorance. Soon the Samaji got up and claimed that he had been defeated. When his disciples wondered how he could have failed when it was Ramakrishna who had been unable to answer a single question, the Samaji, feeling genuinely contrite, replied that Ramakrishna had made him feel small by being so defenceless. Ramakrishna's genuine acknowledgment of his ignorance made the scholar realize how silly he was to fight honesty and simplicity.

True humility does not demand performance or perfection. It allows me to live with my frailties and humaneness.

We are like children building a sandcastle. We embellish it with beautiful shells. The castle is ours, off limits to others. We are willing to attack if others threaten to harm it. Yet, despite all our attachment we are mindful and know that the tide will inevitably come in and sweep the sandcastle away. The trick is to enjoy it fully without clinging and, when the time comes, let it dissolve back into the sea.

Mindful living is about recognising the impermanence of much around us and thus let the impermanence intensify the preciousness of life."

> *"Be an all-out, not a hold-out."*
>
> *- Norman Vincent Peale-*

Chapter Seventeen

> *"You can never get to peace and inner security without first acknowledging all of the good things in your life. If you're forever wanting and longing for more without first appreciating things the way they are, you'll stay in discord."*
>
> - Doc Childre and Howard Martin -

Door Six: The Challenge of Gratitude

The Gift: Self Worth

Know Yourself and Grow Yourself

"Here we are at door six! This door is designed to help us develop an attitude of gratitude, to help us not to take things personally, to accept abundance, and release our fear of greatness. The purpose of this door in Souldrama is to encourage self-worth and to invite you to deeply consider those things for which you are grateful. Each of these objectives is framed within a context of being in the here and now, staying in the present. Here you can see yourself living with purpose and performing your soul's mission. In this phase, your vision expands, imagination is freed, consciousness grows, bondage to the fear and anxiety regarding mortality is vanquished, and the descending spirit unites with the ascending soul.

When we pass through this door, we learn to be open to realize our worth in the world, not to take things personally, and to accept abundance. We can discover a sense of wholeness as we appreciate both the small and big things in our lives continually remaining open to new perspectives. Now that we are able to sustain our non-judgmental awareness, we can become more in touch with our lives as they unfold. Consciousness discovers the divine world, the Divine Self, the permanent, living manifestation of God expressed within and through the human soul, characterized by a stable individual filled with all the qualities the represented in all six doorways so far: Faith, Truth, Compassion, Love, Humility, and Gratitude."

Can an Attitude of Gratitude Help?

"Practicing gratitude is not new. Gratitude is a character strength admired around the globe. From Cicero to Buddha, many philosophers and spiritual teachers have celebrated gratitude. The world's major religions, including Christianity, Judaism, Islam, and Hindu, prize gratitude as a morally beneficial emotional state that encourages reciprocal kindness. In recent years, many scientists have begun examining the links between religion and good health, both physical and mental. Now two psychologists are working to unlock the puzzle of how faith might promote happiness. Dr. Michael McCollough, and Dr. Robert Emmons, say their initial scientific study indicates that gratitude plays a significant role in a person's sense of well-being. "Gratitude is the "forgotten factor" in happiness research. Religions and philosophies have long embraced gratitude as an indispensable manifestation of virtue, and an integral component of health, wholeness, and well-being." (Emmons, 2004).

"McCullough and Emmons (2004) were curious about why people involved with faith seem to have more happiness and a greater sense of well-being than those who aren't and decided to study the connections. The results of the study indicated that daily gratitude exercises resulted in higher reported levels of alertness, enthusiasm, determination, optimism, and energy. Additionally, the gratitude group experienced less depression and stress, was more likely to help others, and made more progress toward personal goals. According to the findings, people who feel grateful are also more likely to feel loved. McCollough and Emmons also noted that gratitude encouraged a positive cycle of reciprocal kindness among people since one act of gratitude encourages another."

Doug: *"Are gratitude and faith tied together?"*

McCullough (2008) says these results also seem to show that gratitude works independently of faith. Though gratitude is a substantial part of most religions, he says the benefits extend to the general population, regardless of faith or lack thereof. In light of his research, McCullough suggests that anyone can increase their sense of well-being and create positive social effects just from counting their blessings. This is in effect what gives us a sense of self worth."

Count Your Blessings

Colleen: *"How can I begin to feel grateful when I am not?"*

"Begin to live in the present and there is some truth to the old saying of count your blessings. Although soul works through individuals, its focus is on the needs of others and on service to humanity. Personal growth can be a long hard journey. Everything in life can be nourishing and everything can bless us, but we've got to be truly present for the blessing to occur. If you are willing to connect deeply and be present with your environment, and tune in with gratefulness, you will find that spirit is everywhere; in your relationships, your work, your daily chores, and in nature.

Gratefulness is the heart of prayer. We can begin to cultivate spiritual wealth by opening our hearts in gratitude and then we can become abundant in spirit. Start a gratitude journal today. Each evening, write down at least five things for which you are grateful. This simple tool will help you open your eyes to the abundance of your world right now.

Lyuobomirsky, Sheldon, and Schkade (2006) argue that one's chronic happiness level is determined partly by a genetic baseline or set point (50%), partly by circumstances (10%), and partly by intentional activity (40%). Practicing gratitude is an intentional activity that can make a real and ongoing difference in chronic happiness levels. Emmons and McCullough (2008) report that people who conduct certain gratitude exercises are healthier and feel better about their lives, make more progress toward goals, are more optimistic, and are more likely to help others than people in control groups. In fact, those who kept gratitude journals on a weekly basis exercised more regularly, reported fewer physical symptoms, felt better about their lives as a whole, and were more optimistic about the upcoming week compared to those who recorded hassles or neutral life events (Emmons & McCullough, 2003). Participants who kept gratitude lists were more likely to have made progress toward important personal goals (academic, interpersonal and health-based) and were more likely to report having helped someone with a personal problem or having offered emotional support to another, relative to the hassles or social comparison condition."

Free the Ego

Maria: *"How can I be open without taking things personally? Everyone always tells me how sensitive I am to every little emotion. My whole life I have been told "You are so sensitive!"*

"First Maria, awareness is the key to all change. Thank you for sharing this with us. Being sensitive is what gives us the ability to be intuitive and creative and is a wonderful thing, not a bad thing. Thank them for the compliment! Perhaps those who told you that wished they were more sensitive!

But, what you are talking about has to do with the concept of containment of your responses which implies the ability to experience what is happening in yourself and others with accepting awareness, without becoming defensive or acting to discharge the tension (Rand, 1996).When we can do this, it becomes a way of providing secure support and honoring another's boundaries. It will help you stop comparing yourself to others and to yourself now as well as to your former self and stop focusing on what you do not have. Each time you judge and compare yourself, you are feeding the ego and the ego loves to be fed. When we free the ego, emotions and thoughts become depersonalized and we stop taking things personally. There is no longer a self in them; our human story no longer defines you and becomes of secondary importance in your history. No longer forming your sense of identity, you become the light of your presence-the awareness of what comes prior to any deep thoughts and emotions."

Iye: *"Then how can we increase the level of gratitude we experience in our jobs and our lives?"*

"There are many facets of work and life in general that we do not control. Remember the serenity prayer we spoke about in the first door of faith? We can increase our control over our own responses to events. One way to raise our overall level of well-being and grow stronger even in the face of trouble and stress is to practice being grateful. To increase gratitude, a good first step is to notice the good things that happen to us, large, and small. These practices can help us take fewer blessings for granted. Here are a few suggestions: These are decisions that we can consciously make each day.

- Establish regular times to focus on being grateful. Gratitude is a character strength that can be enhanced with practice. My favorite time is right before I fall asleep and when I wake up in the morning.

- When facing a loss or a difficult task or situation, remind yourself to be grateful both for what you haven't lost and for the strengths and opportunities that arise from facing difficulties. Tennen and Affleck (found that benefit-seeking and benefit-remembering are linked to psychological and physical health. Benefit finding involves choosing to focus on the positive aspects of the situation and avoiding the feeling of being a victim.

- Elicit and reinforce gratitude in the people around you. Negative moods feed the ego and keep us separate. I like to give someone a compliment each day, especially those close to me that I may take for granted."

Bob piped up: *"I never knew that I was so good being a father until the group chose me to be their ideal father in an exercise."*

"Sometimes, someone else can mirror what is good in your own life and make it visible to you. Let gratitude be your goal."

Iye: *"So gratitude is like the fertilizer for our gardens to give us the seeds of self worth!"*

The Seeds of Self Worth

"Well said! The more we practice gratitude, the more we sow the seeds of self-worth and our gardens will be continuously in bloom. Here are some of those seeds to help our self-worth to bloom.

- Well-Being: Grateful people do not deny or ignore the negative aspects of life. Grateful people report higher levels of positive emotions, life satisfaction, vitality, optimism and lower levels of depression and stress. The temperament toward gratitude appears to enhance pleasant feeling states more than it diminishes unpleasant emotions (McCullough et. al., 2002).

- Prosociality: People with a strong disposition toward gratitude have the capacity to be empathic and to take the perspective of others. They are rated as more generous and more helpful by people in their social networks (McCullough, Emmons, & Tsang, 2002).

- Spirituality: Gratitude does not require religious faith, but faith enhances the ability to be grateful. Those who regularly attend religious services and engage in religious activities such as prayer, and read religious materials are more likely to be grateful. Grateful people are more likely to acknowledge a belief in the interconnectedness of all life and a commitment to and responsibility to others (McCullough et al., 2002).

- Materialism: Grateful individuals place less importance on material goods; they are less likely to judge their own and others success in terms of possessions accumulated; they are less envious of others; and are more likely to share their possessions with others relative to less grateful persons. (McCullough et. al., 2002)."

"Skye tells me every day how much she appreciates me. Sometimes I feel so undeserving. I really have to get used to this!"

"When we appreciate something, it usually means that we have a combination of thankfulness, admiration, and approval. Just like in the financial world, when something appreciates, it grows in value-so it is the same when you remember to appreciate yourself ;your life will grow in value. Gratitude is a character strength admired around the globe. It helps our gardens to bloom. If feel unworthy, you will not be in your true power and so you will be easier to control. I believe that the illusion of feeling unworthy is a condition of being human. Have you ever noticed that it is often easier to pray for someone else before you pray for yourself? Self-worth means remembering to appreciate ourselves. Appreciation is more than just acceptance; it also implies respect and admiration and this is where you can let go of criticism and self-abuse. Ask yourself: Who in your life helps you to tend your garden? God is our constant gardener to help us to bloom where we are planted."

> *"Let us be grateful to people who make us happy; they are the charming gardeners who make our souls blossom."*
> *- M. Proust -*

Chapter Eighteen

> *"If the doors of perception were cleansed, everything would appear ... as it is, infinite."*
>
> *William Blake*

The Challenge of Door Seven: Inspiration

The Gift: Transformation

UQ, Where are You?

"This is the final doorway where you will learn to live in the moment, acknowledge with grace that you are a co creator with God, and realize that transformation may come with laughter. Here you know what you believe in and what motivates you. You are back to the child like state of being in the here and now but with purpose and not impulsivity. Now, we can live in the present ever increasing our spontaneity and creativity. Our mind body and soul are in balance. We feel connected and related to the whole.

We have incorporated the gifts of all three intelligences and gone through the challenges of the previous six doors. Door seven is the door of integration of all three intelligences as well as the gifts that come with the challenges of the doorways. Integration may be regarded as a balancing of intellect, emotions, and intuition. This is known as integrative knowing that results in a universal intelligence or what I like to call a UQ. Each of the doorways has led us through the transitional space leading to transpersonal consciousness where we can see clearly now who we really are."

Iye: "*How does Souldrama relate to my recovery in the Twelve Steps?*"

"Good Question, Iye, Souldrama puts spirituality into action as the Twelve Steps are linked to seven doors of spiritual transformation aligning the ego with the soul.

Souldrama as a Psychotherapeutic Tool to **Prevent** Relapse

"A Twelve-Step program is a set of guiding principles for recovery from addictive, compulsive, or other behavioral problems, originally developed by the fellowship of Alcoholics Anonymous to guide recovery from alcoholism. As summarized by the American Psychological Association, working the Twelve Steps involves the following:

- admitting that one cannot control one's addiction or compulsion;
- recognizing a spiritual higher power that can give strength;
- examining past errors with the help of a sponsor (experienced member);
- making amends for these errors;
- learning to live a new life with a new code of behavior;
- helping others that suffer from the same addictions or compulsions.

The way of life outlined in the 12-steps has been adapted widely by millions of members in recovery from addictions. The same principles are found around the world. What is common in every program is that each step requires taking action, learning new roles, and applying new behaviors. There is a need today to create action techniques in counseling to help prevent relapse that are superior to the feelings of fear, rage, anger, pain, and sadness that maintain dysfunctional roles. The spiritual growth process is achieved by permeating the barriers to the repressed Higher Unconscious (i.e., fear of letting go and surrendering) and embracing it, (Maslow, 1971). This represents an increase in the experience of higher, mystical, and spiritual states of consciousness. With many clients, self-loathing is so great that it impedes forward movement and trust is absent because they feel so alone and afraid. In their world, trust, love, and acceptance come from something outside of themselves such as alcohol, drugs, or a dysfunctional relationship; it is their higher power. Twelve-Step recovery programs help in converting the non-transcending self-actualizers, stuck in their rational intelligence. The next step, Souldrama®, shows how the experiential process of progressing through seven doors of transformation can help a client move toward the transcendent self-actualized state thus reducing relapse while accessing a higher level of spiritual consciousness.

When people embark on a journey of personal growth, they hope to overcome pervasive feelings of fear, addictions, self-hatred, and unworthiness. Becoming identified with mind and emotion can sabotage our relationships, preoccupy our thinking, increase our state of anxiety, and unhappiness and keep us out of a state of joy. As we begin to identify with our minds and emotion, we identify with ego, and any time we become identified with something or label ourselves we feed the ego.

The transition from the level of the ego to the existential requires the ego to de-construct. Adaptive regression in the service of the ego is, in fact, one of the twelve recognized healthy ego functions: the capacity to let go, to suspend controls with pleasure and to permit ideas and fantasies to emerge in a regressed state thus furthering imagination, play, humor, inventiveness, and creativity (Bellak & Goldsmith, 1984).

Psychodrama is the therapeutic modality used within the structure of Souldrama that encourages this to happen. Successive disintegrations are necessary in the developmental process to allow for new growth and for consolidating it. It is a healthy function of the ego called adaptive regression, relaxing secondary thinking, increasing awareness of previously unconscious content, and increasing conscious thinking.

Stage One: Rational Intelligence: What I Think.

In this stage, the ego is very busy trying to define who we think we are and the soul is trying to communicate to the ego who we truly are. Here is how the twelve steps are related to Souldrama.

Door One: Faith

Purpose: To access our faith and to surrender to something higher than ourselves

Goal: To build trust among group members

Corresponding Steps:

Step 1.   Admitted we were powerless over our addiction and that our lives were unmanageable.

Step 2.   Came to believe that a power greater than ourselves could restore us to sanity.

Door Two: Truth

Goal: Clarity of our life's purpose; embrace the shadow

Corresponding Steps:

Step 3.   Made a decision to turn our will and our lives over to the care of God as I understood him.

Step 4.   Made a searching and fearless inventory of ourselves.

Stage Two Emotional Intelligence: What I Feel

Door Three: Compassion
Goal: Forgiveness
Corresponding Steps:

Step 5.   Admitted to God, to ourselves, and another human being the exact nature of wrongs.

Step 6.   We're entirely ready to have God remove all these defects of character.

Door Four: Love
Goal: Unconditional Self-Love
Corresponding Steps:

Step 7.   Humbly asked him to remove our shortcomings.

Step 8.   Made a list of persons we had harmed and became willing to make amends to them all.

Level Three: Spiritual Intelligence, "What I Am"

Door Five: Humility
Goal: Self Empowerment
Corresponding Steps:

Step 9.   Made direct amends to such people except when to do so would injure others.

Step 10.   Continued to take personal inventory and when we were wrong, promptly admitted it.

Door Six: Gratitude
Goal: Self-worth.

Step 11.   Sought through, prayer and meditation, to improve our conscious contact with God, as we understand him, praying only for knowledge of his will for use and the power to carry that out.

Step 12.   Having had a spiritual awakening as the result of this step, we tried to carry this message to those that still suffer and to practice these principles in all our affairs.

Door Seven: Inspiration

Purpose: Inspiration and Co-creativity.

Goal: Transformation and integration of all three intelligences and all twelve steps; being open to the present. Here the group members can see themselves living with purpose and performing their soul's mission. Consciousness discovers the divine world, the Divine Self, the permanent, living manifestation of God expressed within and through the human psyche, characterized by a stable individual filled with all the qualities the Messengers represented in all Six Doors: Faith, Truth, Compassion, Love, Humility, and Gratitude.

In the last Door, members begin to live in the moment, listening to the voice of the soul and becoming co-creators with God. They listen non-defensively and openly, integrating all three spiritual intelligences. They appreciate being in the here and now with purpose instead of impulsivity. They are spontaneously living and are responsive to the current moment, focused on their higher purpose. At this point, members concentrate on the spiritual integration of their experiences and perceptions, express humility, and embrace their uniqueness while understanding their inherent spiritual journey.

Bob: *"How do I stay present?"*

The Present of Being Present

"We live in the present. Personal growth can be a long hard journey. Everything in life can be nourishing. Everything can bless us, but we've got to be truly present for the blessing to occur. This can be a conscious decision that we are invited to make each day. If you are willing to connect deeply and be present with your environment, you will find that spirit is everywhere -- in your relationships, your work, your daily chores, in nature. If you pay attention to what's happening in each moment, you will discover that life continually brings us opportunities to heal our past wounds. When a painful memory surfaces, you can now stay present, and take the time to feel it fully, giving compassion to yourself and others, freeing yourselves to more fully connect with life."

Iye: *"Much of what happened this week seemed mystical. Will we continue to have these experiences and if I do how will I know they are truly mystical?"*

"First, let's look at what I call transcendent experiences. In his classic work that began the modern psychological study of religious experience, William James (1961) identified four qualities of a transcendent experience:

- *ineffability* – the inadequacy of words to express the extraordinary quality of the experience;

- *noesis* –receiving knowledge by direct and instantaneous perception;

- *transiency–* the typically momentary quality of the experience; and

- *passivity* –having little or no control over the experience.

Pahnke and Richards (1972) identify nine core characteristics of mystical experiences.

1. *unity*: internal (the usual sense of individuality falls away) or external (one's identity merges with the sensory world in recognition of an underlying oneness.)

2. *noetic quality of experience*: direct insight into the nature of being, accompanied by the certainty that such knowledge is truly real and not delusion.

3. *transcendence of space and time*: the experience of time and space shifting their usual parameters.

4. *sense of sacredness*: a non rational, intuitive, and quiet response to inspiring realities.

5. *deeply felt positive mood*: feelings of joy, love, blessedness, bliss, and peace.

6. *paradoxicality*: experience of unity of opposites is felt to be true in spite of violating normal logical principles.

7. *ineffability*: the inability to adequately express the experience in everyday language.

8. *transiency*: the transient nature of the experience relative to the apparent permanence of everyday consciousness.

9. *positive change of attitude or behavior:* resulting from having had the experience.

To go further, there are many dimensions of reality below what we normally see and hear. We need to be open to the mystery. In order to be open to mystical experiences, Fitzgerald (1966) suggested that our personalities must have the following components:

- Tolerance for regressive experiences (affects, childishness, fantasy, daydreaming, etc.)

- Tolerance for logical inconsistencies (seeming impossibilities or bizarre implications)

- Constructive use of regression (uses fantasies in a creative way)

- Altered states (inspirational experiences with relative breakdowns of reality orientation)

- Peak experiences (seeks experiences which are overwhelming, enrapturing, and thrilling)

- Capacity for regressive experiences (inquisitive into the unusual, with rich imagination, and not bound by conventional categories of thought)

- Tolerance for the irrational (acceptance of things which violate common sense."

Go With the Flow

"Csikszentmihalyi (1990) also has found evidence of a range of experiences in which people's identities seem to merge with something else where there is a loss of self awareness. These are all states of being. "What slips below the threshold of awareness," he says, "is the concept of self, the information we use to represent to ourselves who we are" (Csikszentmihalyi, 1990, p. xi). You can call these experiences as being in the flow, a joyous and creative total involvement with life. His research has shown that these experiences occur to people in the course of many surprisingly commonplace activities: working, dancing, climbing a mountain, and gardening. For some people, inner anxiety and self-consciousness disappear when they become deeply engaged in such pursuits."

Mary: *"I know that feeling I know this sounds silly but I can go to the beach and look for shells and loose all sense of time. I feel at one with the ocean, sand, and sky."*

Iye: *"Yes, that's how I am when I have my camera. I lose all sense of time."*

"How do we know when we are in the flow? Well, to take this further, Csikszentmihalyi (1990) has broken down the eight components of the experience of being in the flow:

1.   Engagement in a challenge for which the person has the necessary skill to excel.

2.   Absorption in which one's awareness merges with one's actions.

3.   Setting of clear goals that are unambiguous even though they may be complex.

4.   Presence of feedback that the goals are being reached.

5.   Attenuation of one's usual concerns while one is absorbed in the challenge.

6.   Opportunity to exercise control, to be proactively involved.

7.   Loss of self-awareness which involves the sense of individuality melting away ; accompanied by identification or merging with one's environment.

8.   Freedom from the uniform ordering of time, with hours passing by unnoticed.

Each of the states discussed lead to transpersonal consciousness. Gerald May (as cited in Chirban, (2000) quotes), talks about unitive experience as a state in which no self-defining activities take place: "[During the unitive experience] all the activities that serve to define oneself are suspended, yet awareness remains open, clear and vibrant. For the duration of such experiences there is no self-consciousness, no self/other distinction, no trying-to-do or not-to-do, no aspiration, labeling, judgment, or differentiation."

Iye: *"In other words no ego involvement! How do I stay open and connected?"*

"Once you become open to connect with something, you open to its essence, its purpose, and meaning. When our hearts and minds are truly open, we can really hear what's being said or really see what's happening in the moment. Openness demands that we be willing to move to places we've never been before. It asks us to continually challenge the foundations of our belief systems so we can test out new ideas. And to do that, we need to accept insecurity. It means we are continually learning, unlearning and relearning.

Pay attention to good things, large, and small. This often requires intentional thought as well as living in the present because painful things in our lives demand more attention. In my case, I did not know when I outgrew my job or relationships. I was fortunate to suddenly begin to feel a sense of dis-ease and discomfort that something was "not right"..."a feeling that "this is what I have to do," Sometimes, the changes that we make are caused from outside circumstances- a break with relationships, being fired, illness; whatever, the fact remains that a decision has either been made by yourself or others that causes you to move on.

Begin to see each happening and circumstance as a message from God. The secret of successful change is that although the change may look negative on the outside, it is creating a new space for you to grow and develop. Although soul works through individuals, its focus is on the needs of others and on service to humanity. So we will live in a wonderful state of mystery and not see it as something we need to control."

I Can See Can See Clearly Now!

"It takes quite a bit of work to give the positive thoughts in our brain space and not feed the ego."

Carlo: *"With all the pressures of our current lifestyles how can I stay aware not feed the ego? How do I know if I am ego or soul driven?"*

"Many of us wonder the same thing. In the bigger scheme of things, we want our lives to mean something. On the spiritual path, we must be attentive to differentiate whether we are acting from ego or from soul. If ego is in charge, what we do is for our own self-interest. We're looking out for ourselves more than for others. A great way to stay conscious throughout the day is by continually asking yourself about your underlying motivation and intentions of why you are doing what you are doing. Are you doing what you are doing for selfish, manipulative, or fearful reasons, or in honest service? Ask yourself, "Am I doing this because I want to feel worthy? Does my ego want to be fed, noticed and recognized?" If my ego is not convinced that I matter, I may want visible proof that I do by making some kind of impact on life".

Iye: *"How can we feed the soul?"*

"Soul doesn't need recognition or proof that it's worthy. It works through individuals, focusing on the needs of others and on service to humanity. Soul grows the most when it is awake and connected. We need to let go of the pressure we feel from our ego's need to be recognized, It is then that we will be more open and able to simply live soulfully. This is how we will make a difference. Set your intentions high and your life will bloom just life living here in this beautiful land."

Get Cable

"Always remember that your worth does not depend on what you do or how much you have –your worth is in being and not in doing or having. We need to just sit and be. We all have a direct line to God-the problem is the static on the outside and that we have become addicted to the noise. Rather than trying to fix the situation, we must change our perception of the problem. "

Iye: *"So if I begin to live on a spiritual path it will be like getting cable on television instead on just channels 2 and 4?"*

"That is funny, Iye. It's all a matter of identification: Do you identify with the movement of the mind, and with the content of consciousness? Or, are you identifying with the clear, undisturbed background of awareness? Most people do identify with the mind. That is our conditioned habit and pattern. That's why this work is only a matter of unlearning our conditioning so we can begin to see clearly who we really are. Watch for those times when you perceive yourself to be separate from the rest of the world. When we perceive differences in thinking and behaving, we might remember that these are merely different expressions of the one universal life force. We can release judgment as to whether those differences are right or wrong or good or bad. We can drop the labels that divide the world into pieces, and simply appreciate the rich variety of ways that energy can manifest as form."

Oh No! Where Did my Awareness Go?

Iye: *"So does my awareness disappear?"*

"No, it never goes away. Allow your mind to wander and remember that your awareness never will go away even when you forget it. We are really always aware but our minds get in the way. Awareness is always there and constant but when you move from it, you feed the ego and then the mind imagines that your awareness is not there. Our minds are like umbrellas that work best when open."

Bob: *"I truly understand now how come we need to become more aware–so we do not repeat the past,- remain stuck in relationships, live superficial, one dimensional lives, forget experiences of love and beauty, and feel disconnected and isolated from the universe."*

"That is right, Bob. Awareness is sensing deeply and sensitively and when we do this we are fully involved in life. To do this, we need to approach the present as totally new where we can be open and attentive in each moment. This is where we begin to free ourselves from the conditioning of the past and the suffering that it so often brings. As we become more aware, we begin to realize that there's a purpose to everything that happens. This builds our trust, and supports us in being willing to be more open and daring to really experience life as it unfolds.

I see it is raining out. Let's break for lunch and keep our umbrellas and minds open!"

(Back from lunch)

Bill: *"I used to think that everything I needed was outside of me and now I can see how foolish I was. My biggest lesson is that everything I need is right inside of me."*

"When you find yourself longing for something, stop and ask, What is missing from my life? Is it a need? What are the essential qualities of what I seek? How can I experience that now? What's out there? The money you want, the car you want, the job you want, the home you want, the relationship you want? The assumption that "I am going to get what I want out there" is based on scarcity and that you are not enough already. If the message that you are not enough is the one you send out into the universe, the universe will agree with you. When we look for something outside ourselves and try to get more of anything, we stay in a position of lack. Lack is expressed as thinking, I think I am bound by this body, and then I am cut off and separate. Everything is already inside of you; there is no lack. We spend a great deal of time trying to get *it* right -- get the body right, the job right, and the relationship right. The problem is in the trying - the fact that we operate from a "get" mentality."

Living in and Being Responsive to the Moment.

Colleen: *"Now I am getting what living in the now means. I love to tell jokes and make people laugh and have them forget about their problems. My challenge is to stay open and not take things personally. Laughter is a way to stay in the present."*

"Yes, Colleen for when we laugh we are fully present! Let's talk about spontaneity. Here is where we want to acknowledge with grace that you are all co creators with god and that transformation may come with laughter. When we laugh we are able to stay in the present. There is nothing like laughter to bring us back into the moment."

"Sometimes I laugh so hard that I cannot think of anything!"

"As Milton Berle said "Laughter is an instant vacation." How wonderful it is to be in a state of being! Too often, people focus only on results. But getting results without learning something or without having fun are incomplete. Accomplishment is all three: the result, personal growth and having fun.

Moreno (1972) suggested that God acts within the creativity of each individual person. Such creativity and spontaneity is believed to be a connection with God as an expression of transpersonal identification. Rather than being a moralistic God, Moreno (1972) proposed that God encourages aesthetic values which highlight pleasure in creativity, discovery, and celebration of life in the here and now. Therefore God does not act in the role of a judge, but is instead one who invites caring, compassion, and the achievement of our full potential (Moreno, 1972), while we become co-creators. Moreno called spontaneity and creativity the "godhead" in classical psychodrama. He stated that each person has a god-within that can be drawn on as a guide for a creative life and healing force. When our roles become structured or stereotyped as children by our culture, they need to be infused with spontaneity and creativity to be renewed, refreshed, and changed. Moreno's work is the reintegration of spontaneity and creativity. Psychodrama continually focuses the individuals experience to help one change their old, outdated roles learned from their experiences and behaviors. The capacity to take responsibility to change these roles is developed through a number of component abilities such as initiative, improvisation and fearlessness to question the cultural conserve. The elements of spontaneity must be reclaimed and reintegrated to use the tremendous energies that can help serve as a resource for helping us cope with the challenges of a changing world.

Toward the end of his first published book, Who Shall Survive, he described his hope for humanity; the transformation of human consciousness through the integration of creative play, spontaneity, and psychological theory (Blatner, 2000). Moreno's (1946) methodology is a growth model emphasizing individual responsibility and the creating of one's destiny. Unique to psychodrama is the use of primarily role play in therapy to promote joy, enthusiasm, excitement, playfulness, vitality, deep feelings, sharing, and the integration of these emotions with the greater spiritual self. Marsha Sinetar (2000) suggests that children's spirituality thrives on playfulness. It demands respect. And it overflows into the lives of others bringing gifts and abundant riches. She celebrates the spiritual intelligence of children.

Much of Moreno's (1970) work may be understood as being methods and ideas for promoting spontaneity in the service of creativity (Blatner, 1988). In order for spontaneity to occur, a safe and playful environment must exist. Play brings into awareness the child-like aspects of the self which can be a powerful element in integration of fragmented aspects of the psyche. Fully spontaneous enactments help connect everyday mind with deeper soul and spirit. Jung (1958) expanded Freud's view of the subconscious to recognize that it is also a source of innate healing, creativity, and self actualization. Divine energy - spirit -may work in and through our split, complex egos, seeking to bring forth healing. The goal of all psychodramatic treatment is to access, concretize, and experience a spontaneous state of learning and creativity as a healing antidote to past traumatic experiences. Allowing one to travel into the realm of surplus reality allows one to experience developmental repair within and to take a new ending of empowerment."

Co Creation

Maria: *"I have always appreciated how Spirit works with us. I can see more clearly through the group how divine life force partners with our unique perspective, our passion and our skills to create new life situations."*

"That is right. We are not passive vessels for God's will. To realize our highest potential, we must co-create with the divine, as partners in manifestation. Each act of manifestation may be directed toward a specific outcome, but it also contributes to the greater manifestation of the wholeness, love, compassion, and creativity of the primal source from which we all come. When we are in a state of co creation there is a synchronistic and mutually supportive relationship between the inner creative energies of a person's own mind and spirit and their counterpart within the larger world so that we can bring a new and desirable situation into being.

Let's do one last piece of sociometry: please put your hand on the shoulder of the person that you feel has helped you the most this week. The group has formed a circle and everyone has been chosen. We are all connected now and have formed the symbol of unconditional love. Until we journey back through the doorways again, we will live on purpose for life is circular and not linear."

Lao-tzu (1996) said "As long as your shallow worldly ambitions exist, the door will not open".

"Remember, you are not in the universe but the universe is in you. The doorways we went through were inside of us so that our egos could get thin enough to align with the soul. The egos ultimate state of disappointment is enlightenment. The doorways are simply states of consciousness and once you move through them, you will understand that you are bigger than your pain and rest in the state of mystical awareness of who you truly and deeply are. You have a great force within you inspiring you to wake up and recognize the reality of who you are. You can now respond to others from sacredness recognizing that we are the co-creators of our reality and linked to viewing a situation with wonderment, mystery, humility, respect, and gratitude. The sacred response comes from the choice to want to heal others and yourself and from a choice to appreciate the infinite scope of possibilities. Now, we begin to ask the universal mind or IQ, "How may I serve?" Our attention is not focused on ourselves but on the joy that comes from giving and serving and being on our higher purpose. No longer are our responses out of fear and the need for survival in order to create a personal identity, nor from reaction, competition, and power. They are now from vision, intuition, creativity and peace. Wherever you go now, you will be open to see the interconnections, influences, and inter-relationships of things and understand how everything is interconnected. The outside is a reflection of our insides and the lower is a reflection of the higher."

A Call to Action

"This force, the creative power underlying the entire universe, is urging you to create brand new standards of reality or a universal intelligence. The status quo is blind to our creative power. Create a brand new world for yourself, one that meets your deepest needs, and you will help raise the quality of consciousness of the entire world. Therefore, be consciousness, aware and present. To grow in consciousness, we must expand our perspectives on life. The more we work with the universal -- the concept of unity and wholeness, the more everything makes sense. Parts have meaning when they are understood to be parts of a bigger picture. When we serve others with gentleness from our higher purpose we duplicate the energy field from which we all came." (Tolle, 2008)

We have forgotten who we are and how to consciously contact God. Now, you are aware of your higher purpose and can manifest your gifts for others. This is a call to action now for you all to live the spiritual life without any attachment to the results. Spirit does not only work through us, it works with us. Now that we have arrived at the last doorway we will be bringing home the gifts that we have earned, in each doorway. to help others."

Iye: *"I have had such a wonderful time I have never felt so close to anyone before. I will be very sad to leave. Not only have I met the girl of my dreams but I now know myself. I will be moving to this new land and opening the photography business I have been dreaming about."* The others nodded and smiled. *"Skye and I are first going back to the land of Ego to bring back our gifts and hopefully help create a universal intelligence. Summing up what I am leaving with, my spiritual gift from my mother was to give others their space and from my father, the ability to become present and involved. My moment of love was with my dog as a child. These are the gifts that I need to be a great photographer. Gifts I will give to others as I photograph pets and their owners so they will always remember their moments of love together. Thank you so much. I never expected all of this. Do you have a message for us or a final word of wisdom?"*

"I will quote Ram Dass, "The next message you need is right where you are.""

Iye: *"Holy Smoke! I just realized that if I combine the first letter of my name, Iye, and that of Skye's, the word formed is IS; "I" for Iye and "S" for Skye meaning smoke and spirit!"*

"Yes, Iye, when we align ego and soul maybe we do get a sort of "holy smoke." Stay present. This is all there is. Thank you, all, for being here."

"Everything you see has its roots in the unseen world. The forms may change, yet the essence remains the same. Every wonderful sight will vanish; every sweet word will fade, but do not be disheartened. The source they come from is eternal, growing, branching out, giving new life and new joy. Why do you weep? The source is within you, and this whole world is springing up from it."

-Jelaluddin Rumi-

Chapter Nineteen

> *"To me there is no difference between one person and another; I behold all as soul-reflections of the one God. I can't think of anyone as a stranger, for I know that we are all part of the One Spirit."* - Paramahansa Yogananda -

Conclusion

Eckharat Tolle (2008) says "If there are so many seekers, why are there so few finders?"

"Perhaps we've misunderstood the whole concept of a spiritual journey as something that involves "seeking". The term 'seeker' means we are looking for something we believe we do not have now. It places all hope on the future because as a seeker, we haven't yet found our salvation. Tolle (2008) encourages us to experience the truth of who we are by being present right now. If we do that, we don't have to seek anything. We already have everything and can relax and rejoice in the power of being. We, as human beings, have the awareness and power to monitor our own evolutionary process and design our evolutionary path.

Our challenge is to break free of our present concept of reality to create brand new dreams that will bring the ideal to life. As creators, we have no limitations but only endless possibilities. With our dreams and visions we can design and manifest dramatic, profound change. We are God's hands.

The one thing that can remain constant is you. We cannot expect individuals, events, objects, and circumstances to provide the satisfaction we are seeking for they cannot and will not. In fact, with this understanding you will begin recognize that within all the separate aspects of your life, this larger Wholeness is constantly manifesting and when you trust this wholeness, nothing more will ever be needed.

We need to starve the ego so that we can see the light shining within each one of us. The normal rhythm of human development, including spiritual development, involves regularly shedding our layers of knowledge, attachments, and identity to make room for expansion into a larger perspective and identity. The mystics encourage us to regularly and naturally clean house, sloughing off rigid identity (Hart, 2000, p. 159).There is a mystical sense of oneness and unity with all that is. Jung (1978) in his book, *Psychology and the East,* calls it "the transcendent at-one-ment" which connects an individual with the one universal mind. "Does [this] mean that the Mind is 'nothing but' our mind? Or that our mind is the Mind? Assuredly it is the latter." (Jung, 1978, p.126). He concludes, "The soul is assuredly not small, but the radiant Godhead itself." (p. 63). Human consciousness is "the invisible, intangible manifestation of the soul" (p.63), and our purpose is to bring into consciousness the contents that press upward from the unconscious, to "kindle a light in the darkness of mere being." (1968, p. 326)

Larry Dossey (1989) discusses the aversion some people have to the idea of our souls being unlimited and infinitely interconnected with all that is, referring to their objections as "spiritual agoraphobia" (p. 9), i.e., a deep-seated fear of vast open expanses of consciousness. That vastness is referred to in the Zen tradition as an "emptiness of mind." In the Jewish tradition, the Ba'al Shem Tov, founder of the Hasidic movement, called it the "Divine Nothingness" or "the Naught," which "brings new life to this world." (Schatz, 1978).

Health, wholeness, and healing all come from the same root. Today we need new methods of healing. In the course of our spiritual careers, we need knowledge and new skills for our modern roles as spiritual leaders. We need to learn to keep up with the modern world and help others see things in a new way. Souldrama can offer a new way to put spirituality into action to access your own spiritual intelligence. As we remove our own blocks, it will be mirrored in your own world. By bridging the gap within ourselves first, between our rational, emotional, and spiritual intelligences, we can hear the quiet voice of the soul directing us toward our true purpose. As we listen to our soul's voice, we become closer to what we naturally do best in life. We become grateful for the gifts, talents, and skills we offer the world. We aspire to create authentic, mutually empathic relationships. When we tap into our spiritual energy, we experience forgiveness, and know our personal legacies will reflect our higher purpose. As spiritual leaders, we can help others access their own spiritual intelligence; facilitating creative and empathic interactions among those they encounter. This is the time for creatively teaching, healing, and incorporating new action techniques for spiritual growth. This is the time to discover the soul's purpose and to live a life full of joy, transformation, and fulfillment.

There are many possible applications for Souldrama in working with grief, reframing daily spiritual practice, helping the ill, connecting with the elderly, facilitating spirituality in addictions, and providing career or corporate development. In addition, this approach could be particularly applicable for pastoral work, or helping addicted clients disconnect from an addictive higher power and reconnect with a loving higher power.

Although Souldrama was originally designed for codependents and for those from addictive and dysfunctional family systems, it may assist people healing from other issues. While spirituality is accessible to those who seek it, facilitating Souldrama requires training and supervision. In addition, it is necessary that each person who wants to use and develop this method must participate in the complete process to develop their own spiritual intelligence.

One cannot change behavior from insight alone. When you connect to spontaneity and creativity, there is a leap from insight into new action. The concern is not what you know about yourself, but how you can change.

Keep Feeding the Soul

One of therapy's ultimate goals is to restore our ability to care and be cared for in reasonably functional ways, to learn to love, and be loved. We can never forget the experience of love.

"The law of pure love is being fully present. Love supersedes the law of karma. It intervenes in the process by focusing in the present. When anything is initiated in Love in the present, the future of that reality will be purposeful, meaningful, loving and powerful. It is true that we are called to create a better world. But we are first of all called to a more immediate and exalted task: that of creating our own lives. In doing this, we act as co-workers with God. We take our place in the great work of mankind, since in effect the creation of our own destiny, in God, is impossible in pure isolation. Each one of us works out his own destiny in inseparable union with all those others with whom God has willed us to live. We share with one another the creative work of living in the world. And it is through our struggle with material reality, with nature, that we help one another create at the same time our own destiny and a new world for our descendants." - *From Love and Living (Nelson, 1995)*.

So when we align the "I" in our intellectual intelligence with the "S" in our Spiritual Intelligence, we get the word "IS" and that is what living in the present is about. When we integrate all three intelligences we get a "UQ" or universal intelligence.

My vision as a therapist and founder of Souldrama includes the following

1. Educate and train leaders in the model of Souldrama.
2. Apply the challenge of multicultural exchange to this systematic model.
3. Provide educational opportunities for action.
4. Promote health and healing.
5. Build spiritual capitol within corporations.
6. Build global community.
7. Cultivate a compassionate, peaceful and cooperative approach to living.

I see the following as vital opportunities for our conscious evolution, both personally and collectively:

Educate and train leaders in the model of Souldrama. The human family is in the midst of the most significant transformation of consciousness. We are becoming aware that through our own consciousness the universe can know itself. This awareness reveals incredible new potential for our individual and collective humanity. We are affecting our own evolution by everything we do. Educating and training leaders in the model of Souldrama will help to awaken in us the aspiration to become more conscious through subjective practices including psychotherapy, meditation, reflection, prayer, intuition, creativity, and conscious choice making that accelerate our evolution in the direction of unity consciousness and inspire us to deeply align our collective vision, to help others access their spiritual intelligence, remove the resistance in their own lives that is stopping them aspiring to create authentic, mutually empathic relationships and from being on their true purpose.

Apply the challenge of multicultural exchange of this systematic model. At this juncture in human history, urgent global crises challenge us to learn to live sustainably, in harmony and gratitude with one another and with the living universe. The changes required of humanity are broad, deep, and far reaching. Only by acting swiftly and creatively can we birth a planetary culture that will bring well-being to every country. By bringing Souldrama to other countries, this process can help us understand each other and emerge-a story of collaboration, citizen action, dialogue and new understandings driven by unprecedented levels of democratic freedom, multicultural exchange, and access to communication. It is nothing less than the story of our collective evolution.

Provide educational opportunities for action. More enlightened leaders will emerge by educating other trainers in this process. We can work to elevate our capacity for conscious reflection and creative action in our personal lives as well as our collective lives as communities when we recognize that the inner and outer aspects of life evolve together. A dramatic awakening in consciousness will involve an equally dramatic shift in outward aspects of our lives. All individuals should be encouraged to use their gifts to create participatory, responsible and compassionate models of leadership.

Promote Health and Healing. The science of mind-body-spirit health has demonstrated the profound connection between the health of a whole person and the health of the system in which he or she lives. Whole systems healing, respecting both traditional knowledge and modern sciences, must be supported in physical, social, and spiritual domains.

Build spiritual capitol within corporations. Conscious businesses that are aware of the scope, depth, and long-range impacts of their actions are key to achieving sustainability. Business must consciously establish an economic basis for a future of equitably shared abundance. We can build spiritual capitol with our spiritual intelligence. The concept of Spiritual capital can establish a base on which there is mutual trust and communication in organizations.

Build Global Community. The new story is about all of us who share this planet. Together, we can create a culture of peace that eliminates the need for armed conflict, respecting and appreciating the glorious diversity of our human family.

Cultivate a compassionate, peaceful and cooperative approach to living. Through the therapeutic use of Souldrama provide great visionary leadership: Great leadership depends primarily on vision that we can appreciate intellectually, emotionally, and spiritually and is the passion and driving force of our enterprise.

What do "U" imagine when you envision your legacy?

"*There is only one thing more powerful than all the armies of the world, and that is an idea whose time has come.*" -
Victor Hugo -

References

Adams, W. (1995). Revelatory openness wedded with the clarity of unknowing: Psychoanalytic evenly suspended attention, the phenomenological attitude, and meditative awareness. *Psychoanalysis & Contemporary Thought. 18(4),* 463-494.

Ahern, G. (1990). *Spiritual/religious experience in modern society: A pilot study.* Oxford: Alister Hardy Research Centre.

Aknin, L. B., Norton, M. I. & Dunn, E. W. (2009). From wealth to well-being? Money matters, but less than people think. *Journal of Positive Psychology.*

Alcoholics Anonymous, (2007) Microsoft® Encarta® Online Encyclopedia. Retrieved Sept. 24, 2007 from http://encarta.msn.com Â© 1997-2007 Microsoft Corporation. Serenity Prayer.

Alcott, L.M. http://womenshistory.about.com/cs/quotes/a/qu_lm_alcott.htm Retrieved on Sept. 2009.

Antonovosky A. (1987). *Unravelling the Mystery of Health, how people manage stress and stay well.* San Fransico, CA: Jossey-Bass Publications.

Arkowitz, H. (1997). Integrative theories of psychotherapy. In P.L. Wachtel, & S.B. Messer (Eds.).*Theories of Psychotherapy: Origins of Evolution.* Washington, DC: American Psychological Association.

Bandura, A. (1977). *Social Learning Theory.* Englewood Cliffs, NJ: Prentice Hall.

Bateson, G (1979). *Mind and nature: A necessary unity.* New York: Bantam Books.

Beecher, H. W. (1985). *Evolution and Religion.* Reissued by Cambridge University Press.

Bellak, L., & Goldsmith, L. A. (1984). *The Broad Scope of Ego Functions Assessment.* New York: John Wiley & Sons.

Bemak, F. & Young, M. E. (1998). Role of catharsis in group psychotherapy. *International Journal of Action Methods, 50*(4), 157-166.

Berle, M. & Frankel, H. *Milton Berle, an Autobiography*. New York: Dell, 1975.

Biano, I. Portugal. ibanaco@gmail.com.

Blake, W. http://www.brainyquote.com/quotes/authors/w/william_ blake_2.html.

Blatner, A. (1988). Spontaneity. In Foundations of Psychodrama: History, Theory & Practice. New York: Springer.

Blatner, A. (1995). No quotes in reference list "Psychodynamics of Trauma", The Center For Experiential Learning, Ltd. (from the Center's Fall Newsletter) http://members.aol.com/CenterWork.

Blatner, A, & Blatner, A. (1997). *The Art of Play: Helping Adults Reclaim Imagination and Spontaneity*. Philadelphia, PA: Brunner/Mazel-Tayler & Francis.

Blatner, A. (1998). Theoretical foundations of psychodrama [On-line]. Available: www.blatner.com/adam/pdtheory.htm.

Blatner, A. (1998a). Why Process Thought is Relevant: A Psychiatrist's Perspective. Presentation at Silver Anniversary Whitehead Conference, the Center for Process Studies, Claremont, California, August, 1988. www.blatner.com/adam.

Blatner, A. (1999). Psychodramatic methods in psychothearapy. In D. Wiener (Ed.). Beyond Talk Therapy: Using Movement and Expressive Techniques in Clinical Practice. Washington, DC: American Psychological Association Press.

Blatner, A. (1999a). "Re-story-ing the Soul". Keynote presentation to the 1999 ASGPP annual meeting, Philadelphia. www.blatner.com/adam.

Blatner, A. (1999b). "Using Enacted Dialogue to Explore Psychospiritual Issues". Presentation at the International Association for Group Psychotherapy conference in London, August, 1998 and also at the annual meeting of the ASGPP annual meeting, Philadelphia, April 11, 1999. www.blatner.com/adam.

Blatner, A. (2000). *Foundations of Psychodrama*. NY: Springer Publishing Company.

Blatner, A (2006). Spring Issue. Psychodrama as a Spiritual Ritual. www.isdac.com.http://homepage.swissonline.ch/INF-SENSITIVITY

Block, J. H. & Block, J. (1980). The role of ego-control and ego-resiliency in the organization of behavior. In A. Collins (Ed.), *Minnesota Symposium of Child Psychology, 13,* 39-101.

Block, J. (1981). Some enduring and consequential structures of personality. In A. I. Rubin, J. Arnoff, A. M. Barclay, & R. A. Zucker (Eds.), *Further Explorations in Personality* (pp. 27-43), New York: Wiley.

Boyatzis, R., Goleman, D. & Rhee, K. (2000). Clustering competence in emotional intelligence: insights from the emotional competence inventory (ECI). In R. Bar-On & J.D.A. Parker (Eds.): Handbook of emotional intelligence (pp. 343-362). San Francisco, CA: Jossey-Bass.

Boyd-Wilson, B. M., Walkey, F. H., & McClure, J. (2004). Serenity: Much more than just feeling calm. In S. P. Shohov (Ed.). *Advances in Psychology Research, (pp. 35-55),* Nova Science Publishers, Inc.

www.brainbasedbusiness.com Illustration.

Brawn, R. (2000).The formal and the intuitive in science and medicine. In: Atkinson T, Claxton G, Eds. The intuitive practitioner. Buckingham: Oxford University Press.

Bridges, W. (1980). *Transitions: Making Sense of Life's Changes.* Menlo Park, CA: Addison-Wesley.

Briere, J (February 2006). Dissociative symptoms and trauma exposure: specificity, affect dysregulation, and posttraumatic stress. *Journal of Nervous Mental Disorders. 194 (2): 78–82.*Brown, D. P. (1985). Hypnosis as an adjunct to the psychotherapy of the severely disturbed patient: An affective development approach. *International Journal of Clinical and Experimental Hypnosis, 33,* 281-300.

Campbell, J. (1972). *Myths to Live By.* New York: The Viking Press.

Campbell, J. (1973). *The Hero with a Thousand Faces.* Princeton, NJ: Princeton University Press.

Cavalli, T. F. (2002). *Alchemical Psychology: Old Recipes for Living in a New World.* New York: Tarcher/Putnam.

Chandler, C. K., Holden, J. M., & Kolander, C. A. (1992). Counseling for spiritual wellness: Theory and practice. *Journal of Counseling and Development, 71*, 168-175.

Chirban, S. (2000). Oneness experience: Looking through multiple lenses. *Journal of Applied Psychoanalytic Studies, 2(3),* 247-264.

Cholet, L. (Sept 1997). To see the contracted soul expand. *Shambhala Sun.* Available online at

http://www.shambhalasun.com/index.php?option=com_content&task=view&id=2015&Itemid=0.

Chögyam T. (2005). *The Sanity We Are Born With: A Buddhist Approach to Psychology.* Boston, MA: Shambhala Publications.

Chopra, Depak. (2000).*How to Know God.* Random House, Reading, UK.

Corsini, R. (2000). *Handbook of Innovative Psychotherapies.* NY: Wiley/Interscience

Cortright, B. (1997). *Psychotherapy and Spirit: Theory and Practice in Transpersonal Psychotherapy.* Albany, NY: SUNY Press.

Covey, S. R. (1989). *The seven habits of highly effective people.* New York: Simon & Schuster.

Csikszentmihalyi, M. (1990). *Flow: The Psychology of Optimal Experience.* New York: Harper Perrenial.

Csikszentmihalyi, M. (1993). *The Evolving Self: A Psychology for the Third Millennium.* New York: Harper Collins.

Dalai Lama. (1997). In F. J. Varela (Ed.), *Sleeping, Dreaming, and Dying: An exploration of Consciousness with the Dalai Lama,* Boston, MA: Wisdom Publications.

Dalai Lama. (1998). Levels of consciousness: From deep sleep to enlightenment. In E. J. Rosen (Ed.), *Experiencing the Soul: Before Birth, During Life, and After Death,* 123-126. Carlsbad, CA: Hay House Inc.

Damasio A. (1994*). Descartes Error.* New York: Putnam.

Dass, Ram. (1998). 'Being' in the moment. In E. J. Rosen (Ed.), *Experiencing the Soul: Before Birth, During Life, and After Death,* 157-167. Carlsbad, CA: Hay House, Inc.

Dayton, T. (1995). *The Living Stage*. Deerfield Beach, Florida. Health Communications.

Dayton, T. (1995). *The Quiet Voice of the Soul.* Deerfield Beach, Florida: Health Communications.

Dayton, T. (1994). *The Drama Within*. Deerfield Beach, Florida: Health Communications.

Dayton, T. (2000). *Trauma and Addiction*. Deerfield Beach, Florida. Health Communications.

Dayton, T. (2008) *Emotional Sobriety: From Relationship Trauma to Resilience and Balance.*

http://tiandayton.com/articles/paradigm_magazine_emotional_sobriet y.pdf.

Dayton, T. (2009). http://www.tiandayton.com/articles/EmotionalRepairThroughActionM ethods.pdf.

Decker, L. R. (1993). Beliefs, post-traumatic stress disorder and mysticism. *Journal of Humanistic Psychology*, *33*(4), 15-32.

Deikman, A. J. (online). *The Spiritual Heart of Service* [available at http://www.deikman.com/spirserv.html].

Deslauriers, D. (2000). Dreamwork in the light of emotional and spiritual intelligence. *Advanced Development, 9,* 105-122.

Doc Childre and Howard Martin. www.heartquotes.net/emotions.html.

Don Miguel Ruiz. (1999). *The Mastery of Love: A Practical Guide to the Art of Relationship* (Toltec Wisdom Book), Amber-Allen Publishing.

Dossey, L (1993). *Healing Words: The Power of Prayer and the Practice of Medicine.* San Francisco: Harper.

Drob, S. L. (1999). The depth of the soul: Hillman's vision of psychology. *Journal of Humanistic Psychology*, *39*(3), 56-72.

Easwaran, E. (1996). *Words to Live By: A Daily Guide to Leading an Exceptional Life.* Nilgiri Press.

Eadie, B. (2001). *Embraced By the Light Prayers and Reflections.* Seattle, Wa.:Onjinjinkta Publishing.

Eddinger, E. F. (1972). *Ego and archetype: Individuation and the religious function of the psyche.* New York: G. P. Putnam's Sons.

Edwards N, Kornacki MJ, Silversin J. Unhappy doctors: what are the causes and what can be done? BMJ 2002;324:835-8.

Eigen, M. (Sum 1992). The fire that never goes out. Psychoanalytic Review, 79(2), 271-287.

Einstein, A. http://rescomp.stanford.edu/~cheshire/EinsteinQuotes.html.

Eisman, J. (Winter 1989). The child state of consciousness and the formation of the self. Hakomi Forum, Issue 7.

Eliade, M. (1977). *From Primitives to Zen: A Thematic Sourcebook of the History of Religions.* San Francisco, CA: Harper & Row.

Elkins, D. N., Hedstrom, L. J., Hughes, L. L., Leaf, J. A., & Saunders, C. (1988). Toward a humanistic phenomenological. Spirituality: Definition, description, and measurement. *Journal of Humanistic Psychology, 28(4),* 5-18.

Emmons, R.A., & McCullough, M.E. (Eds.). (2004). *The Psychology of Gratitude.* New York: Oxford University Press.

Emmons, R.A. (2004). Gratitude. In M.E.P. Seligman & C. Peterson (Eds.), *Character Strengths and Virtues* (pp. 553-568). New York: Oxford University Press.

Engler, J. (1999). Practicing for awakening, Part II. *Insight Journal, vol. 12.*

Erikson, E. H. (1958). *Young Man Luther.* London: Faber & Faber, Ltd.

Fisher, G. (2005). Existential psychotherapy with adult survivors of sexual abuse. *Journal of Humanistic Psychology, 45(1),* 10-40.

Fischer, R. (1975-76). On the remembrance of things present. *Journal of Altered States of Consciousness, 2(4)*, 361-369.

Fischer, R., & Landon, G. M. (Feb 1972). On the arousal state-dependent recall of "subconscious"experience: Stateboundness. *British Journal of Psychiatry, 120(555)*, 159-172.

Fitzgerald, E. T. (1966). Measurement of openness to experience: A study of regression in the service of the ego. *Journal of Personality and Social Psychology, 4*, 655-663.

Fonagy, P., Steele, H., Higgitt, A., & Target, M. (1994). The theory and practice of resilience. *Journal of Child Psychology and Psychiatry*, *35*, 231-257.

Frankl, V.E. (1992). *Man's Search for Meaning.* Boston, MA: Beacon Press.

Frankl, V. E. (1997). *Man's Search for Ultimate Meaning.* Cambridge, MA: Perseus Books.

Freud, A. (1965). The concept of developmental lines. In *The Writings of Anna Freud Vol. 6*, 62-107.New York: International Universities Press.

Gardner, H. (1983). *Frames of Mind: A Theory of Multiple Intelligences.* New York: Basic Books.

Gardner, H. (1999). *Intelligence Reframed.* New York: Basic Books. Gawain, S. (2002). *Creative Visualization: Use the Power of Your Imagination to Create What You Want in Your Life.* California: Nataraj Publishing.

Gazzaniga, M. S. & Sperry, R. W. Language after section of the cerebral commissures. *Brain*, 1967, *90, (I),* 131-148).

Gillham, J.E., & Seligman, M.E.P. (1999). Footsteps on the road to positive psychology. Behaviour Research and Therapy, *37,* S163-S173.

Goleman, D. (1972). The Buddha on meditation and states of consciousness, Part I: The teachings. *Journal of Transpersonal Psychology, 4(1),* 1-44.

Goleman, D. (1995). *Emotional intelligence.* New York: Bantam Books.

Goleman, D. (1998). *Working with emotional intelligence.* New York: Bantam Books.

Greenberg, J. R., & Mitchell, S. A. (1983). *Object Relations in Psychoanalytic Theory.* Cambridge, Ma: Harvard University Press.

Greenhalgh T. Intuition and evidence: uneasy bedfellows? Br J Gen Pract. 2002*;52*:395-400.

Greenspan, S.T. &. Benderly,B.L.(1997) *The Growth of the Mind: And the endangered origins of intelligence.* Massachusetts: Perseus Books.

Grosso, M. (1998). Theta consciousness: Survival research with the living. In E. J. Rosen (Ed.),*Experiencing the Soul: Before Birth, During Life, and After Death*, 261-264. Carlsbad, CA: Hay House Inc.

Harding, E. M. (1965). *The I and the Not I: A study of the development of consciousness*. Princeton, NJ: Princeton University Press.

Harding, M. E. (1973). *Psychic Energy: Its Source and Its Transformation*. Princeton, NJ: Princeton University Press.

Hartman, D., & Zimberoff, D. (2003). The existential approach in Heart-Centered therapies. *Journal of Heart-Centered Therapies, 6(1),* 3-46.

Hartman, D., & Zimberoff, D. (2004). Existential Resistance to Life: Ambivalence, Avoidance & Control. *Journal of Heart-Centered Therapies, 7(1),* 3-63.

Hasidic Saying. (http://www.cheraglibrary.org/heart/heart1-2.htm).

Heidigger,M. (1971). *On the Way to Language.* San Francisco, Ca. Harper Collins.

Hillman, J. (1978). *Re-Visioning Psychology.* Perennial.

Hillman, R. G. (1981). The psychopathology of being held hostage. *American Journal of Psychiatry, 138,* 1193–1197.

Holy Bible.(2000), Proverbs 23:7. Giant Print Presentation Edition: King James Version. Publisher: Oxford University Press, USA.

Hugo, V. http://www.brainyquote.com/quotes/authors/v/victor_hugo_8.html.

Jacobi, J. (1965). *The Way of Individuation*, Trans. by R.F.C. Harcourt, Brace & World, New York, NY.

Jaques, E. (1965). *A General Theory of Bureaucracy.* Heinemann Gower. Portsmouth, NH.

Jaques, E. (1996). *Requisite Organization: A Total System for Effective Managerial Organization and Managerial Leadership for the 21st Century.* 2nd Ed., Cason Hall, Falls Church, VA.

Jaques, E. and Cason, K. (1994). *Human Capability*. Cason Hall, Falls Church, VA.

James, W. (1890). *Principles of Psychology.* New York: Henry Holt.

James, W. (1961). *The Varieties of Religious Experience: A Study in Human Nature*. New York: Macmillan Publishing Co. (Original work published in 1902).

Jeffries, J. (1998). The processing. In M. Karp, P. Holmes, & K. Bradshaw-Tauvon (Eds.), Handbook of Psychodrama, 189-202. London: Routledge.

Johnson, D. R. (1999). Essays on the Creative Arts Therapies. Springfield, IL: Charles C. Thomas.

Jung, C. G. (1933). *Modern Man in Search of a Soul*. New York: Harcourt Brace Jovanovich.

Jung, C. G. (1934). *The Meaning of Psychology for Modern Man. Collected Works, Vol. 10*. Princeton, NJ: Princeton University Press.

Jung, C.G. (1955; FEBRUARY)) The Old Wise Man, TIME MAGAZINE .

Jung, C. G. (1958). *Psyche and Symbol*. New York: Doubleday.

Jung, C. G. (1959). *The Archetypes and the Collective Unconscious*. Princeton, NJ: Princeton University Press.

Jung, C. G. (1961). *Memories, Dreams, Reflections*. New York: Vintage.

Jung, C. G. (1966). *Two Essays on Analytical Psychology*. Princeton, NJ: Princeton University Press.

Jung, C. G. (1978). *Psychology and the East*, R. F. C. Hull, trans. Princeton, NJ: Princeton University Press.

Jung, C. G. (1996). *The Psychology of Kundalini Yoga: Notes of the Seminar Given in 1932 by C. G.Jung*, Sonu Shamdasani (Ed.). Bollingen Series XCIX. Princeton, NJ: Princeton University Press.

Jung, Karl, (2007) http://www.oktm.ca/Quotes_content-I.htm.

Jung, C. G. & von Franz, M.L. (1964). *Man and his symbols*. Garden City, NY: Doubleday.

Kalsched, D. (1996). *The Inner World of Trauma*. London: Routledge.
Kalsched, D. E. (2003; ARPIL). Daimonic elements in early trauma. *Journal of Analytical Psychology, 48*(2), 145-169.

Kaufman, G. D. (1981). *The Theological Imagination: Constructing the Concept of God*. Philadelphia, PA: Westminster.

Keller, H. http://www.brainyquote.com/quotes/authors/h/helen_keller_3.html.

Keutzer, C. S. (1978). Whatever turns you on: Triggers to transcendent experiences. *Journal of Humanistic Psychology*, 18(3), 77-80.

Khavare, K. (1995). *Spiritual Intelligence*. Ontario, Canada: White Mountain Publications.

Kierkegaard, S., Hong, H.,& Hong, E.(2000). *The Essential Kierkegaard*. Princeton, N J: Princeton University Press.

Kirkpatrick, L. A. (1999). Attachment and religious representations and behavior. In J. Cassidy & P. R. Shaver (Eds.), *Handbook of Attachment: Theory, Research, and Clinical Applications*, 803-822. New York: Guilford Press.

Kirkpatrick, L. A., & Shaver, P. (1992). An attachment theoretical approach to romantic love and religious belief. *Personality and Social Psychology Bulletin*, 18, 266-275.

Kohut, H. (1971). *The Analysis of the Self: A Systematic Approach to the Psychoanalytic Treatment of Narcissistic Personality*. New York: International Universities Press.

Kravitz, Y yaacov@spiritualintelligence.com. Spiritual Intelligence® is registered nationally as a Service Mark in the U.S. Patent and Trademark Office, since March 2000. © Yaacov J. Kravitz, 2002. All rights reserved.

Laing, R. D. (1960). *The Divided Self*. London: Tavistock.

Laing, R. D. (1968). *The Politics of Experience*. New York: Ballantine.

Langenscheidts Dictionary. (1999). Langenscheidt Publishers Inc., New York.

Lao-Tzu & Walker, B. (1996). *The Tao Te Ching of Lao Tzu*. N.Y.: St. Martin's Griffin.

Laski, M. (1961). *Ecstasy: A Study of Some Secular and Religious Experiences*. London: Cresse).

Levine, S. (1998). *A Year to Live*. Random House: New York.

Lewis, T, Aminin, F & Lannon, R.(2001)*A General Theory of Love.* United Kingdom: Vintage Books.

Lowe, M. C. (2000). Using heart-centered awareness and transpersonal archetypal images as resources supporting post-ego development. *Dissertation Abstracts International: Section B: the Sciences &Engineering, 60(*12-B), 6349.

Maslow, A. (1943). A theory of human motivation. *Psychological Review, 50*, 370-396.

Maslow, A. (1954). *Motivation and Personality.* New York: Harper.

Maslow, A. (1968). *Toward a Psychology of Being. (2nd Ed).* Princeton, NJ: Van Nostrand.

Maslow, A. (1971). *The Farther Reaches of Human Nature.* New York: The Viking Press.

Maslow, A. (1987). *Motivation and Personality* (3rd Ed.). New York: Harper Row.

May, R. (1969). *Love and Will.* New York: Dell.

Mayer, J.D. & Salovey, P. (1997). What is emotional intelligence? In [P. Salovey & D. Sluyter (eds.): Emotional development and emotional intelligence: educational applications (pp. 3-31). New York: Basic Books.

McMullen B. Cognitive intelligence. BMJ 2002; *10:458*-9. , 1951

McMullen B. Emotional intelligence. BMJ 2003; *11:18*-9.

Merton, T. (1985). *Love and Living.* Boston, Ma. Mariner Books.

Miller, C. (2000). The technique of Souldrama and its applications. The International Journal of action methods, *52*, (no 4), 173-186.

Miller, C. (2004). *Souldrama: a Journey into the Heart of God.* Self published. NJ (3rd edition) Lulu.

Miller, C. (2006).Souldrama®: A Therapeutic Action Model to Create Spiritually Intelligent Leadership,Vistas online. http://counselingoutfitters.com/VISTAS_2006.htm.

Miller, C. (2007). *Souldrama: A terapia da alma*: Editora Agora; Sao Paulo, Brazil

Miller, C. (2007). Souldrama®: A therapeutic action model to create spiritually intelligent leadership. The Korean Association for Psychodrama & Sociodrama. *10(1)*, 45-80.

Miller, C. (2007). *Psychodrama: Advances in theory and practice.* In C. Baim, J. Burmeister, M. Maciel (Eds.), Advancing theory in therapy: Psychodrama, spirituality and Souldrama® (pp. 189-200). London: Routledge Press.

Miller, C. (2008). Spirituality in Action. Journal for Creativity in Mental Health. Volume: *3 Issue: 2 ISSN*: 1540-1383 Pub Date: 7/31/2008. Taylor Francis Group.

Miller, C. (2009) The Light Messengers of Souldrama copyrighted by The International Institute of Souldrama.

Miller, C. (2009) From Fearship to Friendship. Live Positive Magazine. April.

Miller, C. (2009) Taking the I out of the IQ. Recovery View Online. http://recoveryview.com/2009/01/letting-go-of-the-%e2%80%9ci%e2%80%9d-in-the-iq-accessing-our-spiritual-intelligence.

Mitroff, I., Mason, R. O., & Pearson, C. M. (1994). Radical surgery: What will tomorrow's organizations look like? *Academy of Management Executive, 8,* 11–21.

Moore, T. (1998). In conversation with Thomas Moore: The soul's mysteries. In A. A. Simpkinson &C. H. Simpkinson (Eds.), *Soul Work: A Field Guide for Spiritual Seekers*, 43-45. New York: Harper Collins.

Moore, T. (1992) Our Soul Odyssey. From *Original Self: Living with Paradox and Authenticity.* Thomas

Moore. Retrieved from website http://www.gracecathedral.org/enrichment/excerpts/exc_20000329.shtml.

Moreno, J. L. (1946). *Psychodrama: Vol 1.* Beacon, NY: Beacon House.

Moreno, J. L. (1971). Psychodrama. In H. I. Kaplan, & B. J. Sadock, (Eds.), Comprehensive group psychotherapy, 460-500. Baltimore, MD: Williams & Wilkins.

Moreno, J. L. (1972). The religion of God-Father. In P.E. Johnson, (Ed.), *Healer of the Mind: A Psychiatrist's Search for Faith.*, (pp. 197-215), Nashville, TN: Abbington.

Moreno, Z. (1965). Psychodramatic rules, techniques and adjunctive methods. *Group Psychotherapy,* 18, 73-86.

Moreno, Z, Blomkvist,L. & Rutzel,T., (2000).*Psychodrama, Surplus Reality and the Art of Healing.* London, Routledge.

Morris, T.(1997). *If Aristotle ran General Motors.* New York: Henry Holt and Company.

Mother Theresa.
http://www.brainyquote.com/quotes/quotes/m/mothertere106501.html
Neal, J. A. (1997). Spirituality in management education: A guide to resources. *Journal of Management Education, 21,* 121–39.

Nelson, M. (1995). *Coming Home: The Return to True Self.* Ca.:Nataraj Pub.

New York Times Illustration. (2005). printed with permission of the New York Times Magazine Cover. Feb. 17, 2005.

Oriah Mountain Dreamer. The Invitation.
http://www.oriahmountaindreamer.com.

Pachter M. Paracelsus. (1951). *Magic into Science.* New York: Schuman.

Pahnke, W. N., & Richards, W. A. (1972). Implications of LSD and experimental mysticism. In C.T.Tart (Ed.), *Altered States of Consciousness*, 409-439. Garden City, NY: Anchor.

Peck, M. S. (1993). *Further along the road less traveled: The unending journey toward spiritual growth.* New York: Simon & Schuster.

Progoff, I.(1992). At a Journal Workshop: Writing to Access the Power of the Unconscious and Evoke Creative Ability. In Nelson, J. (2009) Psychology, Religion, and Spirituality. New York: Springer.Paramahansa Yogananda. (1998). *Autobiography of a Yogi.* Los Angeles, Ca: Self Realization Fellowship.

Proust, M. http://www.brainyquote.com/quotes/authors/m/marcel_proust.html.

Ramachandran, V. & Blakeslee,S (1998) *Phantoms in the Brain: Probing the Mysteries of the Human Mind* .N.Y.: Quill William Morrow.

Rand, M. L. (1996). As it was in the beginning: The significance of infant bonding in the development of self and relationships. *Journal of Child and Youth Care, 10(4),* 1-8.

Roll, W. G. (1968). Some physical and psychological aspects of a series of poltergeist phenomena. Journal of the American Society for Psychical Research, *62*, 263-308.

Rosen, S. (1982). My *Voice Will Go With You: The Teaching Tales of Milton H. Erickson, M.D.* New York; Norton.

Rowan, J. (2005) . *The Transpersonal. Spirituality in Psychotherapy and Counselling* London, UK: Routledge.

Roberts, K. T., & Whall, A. (Win 1996). Serenity as a goal for nursing practice. IMAGE: Journal of Nursing Scholarship, 28(4), 359-364.

Roof, W. C. (1993). *A Generation of Seekers: The spiritual journeys of the baby boom generation.* San Francisco: Harper Collins.

Rumi, J., Green, M. & Barks, C. (1997). *The Illuminated Rumi.*N.Y : Doubleday Dell.

Salovey, P. & Grewal, D. (2005) The Science of Emotional Intelligence. Current directions in psychological science. (*14* -6).

Satir, V. (1988). *The New Peoplemaking.* Palo Alto, CA: Science and Behavior Books.

Scaer, Robert (2001*). The Body Bears the Burden: Trauma, Dissociation, and Disease.* Binghamton, NY: Haworth Medical Press. pp. 97–126. http://books.google.ca/books?id=C30EbO7GDMIC& pg=PA97

Scholem, G. (1941). *Major Trends in Jewish Mysticism.* New York: Schocken.

Schwartz, H. L. (2000). *Dialogues with Forgotten Voices: Relational Perspectives on Child Abuse, Trauma and Treatment of Dissociative Disorders.* New York: Basic Books.

Schwartz, R. C. (1999). Releasing the soul: Psychotherapy as a spiritual practice. In F. Walsh (Ed.), *Spiritual Resources in Family Therapy*, 223-239. New York: Guilford Press.

Shaw, A., Joseph, S., & Linley, P. A. (March 2005). Religion, spirituality, and posttraumatic growth: a systematic review. *Mental Health, Religion & Culture, 8(1),* 1 - 11.

Shengold, L. (1999). *Soul Murder Revisited: Thoughts about Therapy, Hate, Love, and Memory.* New Haven, CT: Yale University Press.

Shoham, S. G. (1990). The Bridge to Nothingness: Gnosis, Kabbala, Existentialism, and the Transcendental Predicament of Man. *ReVISION, 13*(1), 33-45.

Siegel,B. (1986*). Love, Medicine & Miracles: Lessons Learned about Self-Healing from a Surgeon's Experience with Exceptional Patients.* N.Y.: Quill.

Simpkinson, A. A., & Simpkinson, C. H. (1998). *Soul Work: A Field Guide for Spiritual Seekers.* New York: Harper Perennial.

Sinetar, M.(2000)Spiritual Intelligence: *What We Can Learn from the Early Awakening Child.* N.Y:Orbis Books.

Singer, J. (1972). *Boundaries of the soul: The practice of Jung's psychology.* Garden City, NY: Doubleday.

Small, G. (2008). *I Brain: Surviving the Technological Alteration of the Modern Mind.* United Kingdom: William Marrow.

Sogyal Rinpoche. (1993). *The Tibetan Book of Living and Dying.* San Francisco: HarperCollins.

Sperry, R. W. (1961). Cerebral organization and behavior. *Science, 133*, 1749-1757.

Sperry, R. W. & Gazzaniga, M. S. (1967).Language following disconnection of the hemispheres. In: C. H. Millikan & F. L. Darley (Eds.), *Brain Mechanisms Underlying Speech and Language.* New York: Grune & Stratton, Inc., 177-184.

Sperry, R. W., Gazzaniga, M. S. & Bogen, J. E. Interhemispheric relationships: the neocortical commissures; syndromes of hemisphere disconnection. In: P. J. Vinken & G. W. Bruyn (Eds.), *Handbook of Clinical Neurology* (p. 177-184). Amsterdam: North-Holland Publishing Company.

Spiegel, D. (1997). Trauma, dissociation, and memory. In R. Yehuda & A. C. McFarlane (Eds.),*Psychobiology of Posttraumatic Stress Disorder, Annals of the New York Academy of Sciences,* (p. 225-237), New York: New York Academy of Sciences.

Srinath, TT. http://www.thehindubusinessline.com/life/2008/11/07/stories/2008110750110400.htm

St. Augustine. http://www.brainyquote.com/quotes/authors/s/saint_augustine.html

St. John of the Cross. (1959). *The Dark Night of the Soul.* Trans. E. A. Peters. Garden City, NY: Doubleday and Co.

St. Teresa of Avila. (1980). The Interior Castle in K. Kieran & O. Rodriguez(Trans.). *The Collected Works of St. Teresa of Avila, Vol. 2.,* Washington, DC: Institute of Carmelite Studies.

Stein, M. & Hollwitz, J. (1992). *Psyche at work: Workplace applications of Jungian*

analytical psychology. Wilmette, IL: Chiron Publications.

Tedeschi, R. G.& Calhoun, L. G. (1996). The Posttraumatic Growth Inventory: Measuring the positive legacy of trauma. *Journal of Traumatic Stress, 9,* 455-471.

Tedeschi, R. G., & Calhoun, L. G. (Jan 2004). Posttraumatic growth: Conceptual foundations and empirical evidence. *Psychological Inquiry, 15(1),* 1-18.

Thalbourne, M. A. (2000). Relation between transliminality and openness to experience. *Psychological Reports, 86,* 909-910.

Thayer, S. (Speaker). (1997). *Healing with the energy of angels* [Cassette Recording].Holmdel, NJ: The Center of Being, Inc.

Tolle, E.(2008). *A New Earth: Awakening to Your Life's Purpose.* Penguin Books: NY.

Tronick, E. Z. (1989). Emotions and emotional communication in infants. *American Psychologist, 44*(2), 112-119.

Tulku, T. (2000). Lucid dreaming: Exerting the creativity of the unconscious. In G. Watson & S.Batchelor (Eds.), *The Psychology of Awakening: Buddhism, Science, and Our Day-to-Day Lives,* 271-283. York Beach, ME: Samuel Weiser, Inc.

Updegraff, J. A.(2000). Female responses to stress: Tend and befriend, not fight or flight. *Psychological Review, 107(3),* 411-429.

Vaillant, G. (1993). *The Wisdom of the Ego.* Cambridge, MA: Harvard University Press.

Van Kaam, A. (Feb 1994). Transcendent formation. *Journal of Spiritual Formation, 15(1),* 9-20.

Villoldo, A. (2005). *Mending the Past and Healing the Future with Soul Retrieval.* Carlsbad, CA: Hay House Inc.

Van der Kolk BA, Pelcovitz D, Roth S, Mandel FS, McFarlane A, Herman JL *(July 1996).* "Dissociation, somatization, and affect dysregulation: the complexity of adaptation of trauma". *Am J Psychiatry 153 (7 Suppl): 83–93.* PMID 8659645. http://ajp.psychiatryonline.org/cgi/pmidlookup?view=long&pmid=865 9645. Retrieved on 2008-05-13.

Von Franz, M. L. (1964). The process of individuation. In C. G. Jung (Ed.), *Man and his Symbols,* 158-229. Garden City, NY: Doubleday & Company.

Waldron, J. L. (1998). The life impact of transcendent experiences with a pronounced quality of noesis. *Journal of Transpersonal Psychology, 30(2),* 103-134.

Ware, K. (Summer 1997). Discovering the inner kingdom: The prayer of the heart, part two. *Heart Beat, 1,* 8-9.

Washburn, M. (1990). Two patterns of transcendence. *ReVISION, 13,* 3-15.

Washburn, M. (1995). *The Ego and the Dynamic Ground: A Transpersonal Theory of Human Development.* Albany, NY: State University of New York Press.

Weldwood, J. (1976). Exploring mind: Form, emptiness, and beyond. *Journal of Transpersonal Psychology, 8(2),* 89-99.

Weldwood, J.(1990) *Journey of the Heart: Intimate Relations and the Path to Love.* London: Mandala.

Wickapedia. http://en.wikipedia.org/wiki/Humility

Wilber, K. (1977). *The Spectrum of Consciousness.* Wheaton, IL: Quest.

Wilber, K. (1998). *The Eye of Spirit*. Boston, Ma: Shambhala Publications.

Wilber, K. (2000). *Integral Psychology: Consciousness, Spirit, Psychology, Therapy*. Boston, Ma:Shambhala Publications.

Wilson, W. http://www.aaspirit.com/emot-wilson.html

Winnicott, D. W. (1945). Primitive emotional development. *International Journal of Psychoanalysis*, *26*, 137-143.

Winnicott, D. W. (1957). *Mother and Child: A Primer of First Relationships*. New York: Basic Books.

Winnicott, D. W. (1958). *Collected Papers*. New York: Basic Books.

Winnicott, D. W. (1965a). Ego integration in child development. In *The Maturational Processes and the Facilitating Environment*, 61. New York: International Universities Press.

Winnicott, D. W. (1965b). The theory of the parent-infant relationship. In *The Maturational Processes and the Facilitating Environment*, 37-55. New York: International Universities Press.

Winnicott, D. (1965c). Dependence in infant-care, child-care, and in the psychoanalytic setting. In *The Maturational Processes and the Facilitating* Environment, (pp. 249-259), New York: International University Press.

Winnicott, D. W. (1971). *Playing and Reality*. London: Routledge.

Winnicott, D. W. (1989a). Fear of breakdown. In C. Winnicott, R. Shepherd, & M. Davis (Eds.), *D. W.Winnicott: Psycho-analytic Explorations*. Cambridge, MA: Harvard University Press.

Winnicott, D. W. (1989b) On the basis of self in body. In C. Winnicott, R. Shepherd, & M. Davis (Eds.), *D. W. Winnicott: Psycho-analytic Explorations*, 261-283. Cambridge, MA: Harvard University Press.

Whitehead, T. (Autumn 1994). Boundaries and psychotherapy Part I: Boundary distortion and its consequences. *Hakomi Forum*, issue 10.

Whitfield, C. L. (1993). *Boundaries and Relationships: Knowing, Protecting and Enjoying the Self*. Deerfield Beach, FL: Health Communications.

Whitfield, C. L. (1995). The forgotten difference: Ordinary memory versus traumatic memory. *Consciousness and Cognition, 4*, 88-94.

Wolman, R. N. (2001). *Thinking with Your Soul: Spiritual Intelligence and Why It Matters*. New York: Harmony Books.

Woodman, M. (1993). Stepping over the threshold: Into the black hole at the center of Self. *Noetic Sciences Review, 28*, 10-15.

Wuthnow, R. (1978). Peak experiences: Some empirical tests. *Journal of Humanistic Psychology, 18(3)*, 59-75.

Wei, W. (1963). *Ask the Awakened: The Negative Way*. Boston, Ma: Little Brown.

Yalom, I. D. (1975). The Theory and Practice of Group Psychotherapy NY: Basic Books.

Zimberoff, D. & Hartman, D. (1999). Heart-centered energetic psychodrama. *Journal of Heart-Centered Therapies, 2*(1), 77-98.

Zimberoff, D. & Hartman, D. (2007). Posttraumatic growth and thriving with heart centered therapies. *Journal of Heart-Centered Therapies, 10*, 272–288.

Zohar D.& Marshall I (2000). *SQ: Connecting with Our Spiritual Intelligence*. London, England: Bloomsbury Publishing.

Zohar D, & Marshall I.(2003) *SQ—the Ultimate Intelligence*. London: Bloomsbury.

Zohar, D. (2005; FALL). "Spiritually Intelligent Leadership". *Leader to Leader. 38* 45-51.

About the Author

Connie Miller TEP, NCC, LPC, ACA, developed Souldrama® as a group action method that accesses our spiritual intelligence by balancing our rational, emotional and spiritual intelligences so that we can live on purpose and become spiritually intelligent leaders. This is a model that involves aligning the ego and soul by passing through seven stages of transformation. An author of many international articles, as well as being a contributor to the book, New Advances in Psychodrama, Routledge (2009), her articles and books have been published in Korean and Portuguese. Connie lives in the USA and is Trainer, Educator and Practitioner of psychodrama, sociometry and group psychotherapy, Licensed Professional Counselor and Nationally Certified Counselor. She runs workshops, lectures and trains people worldwide through the International Institute of Souldrama. A recipient of the 2009 innovators award for Souldrama, from the American Society of Psychodrama, Group Psychotherapy, and Sociometry, Connie has presented Souldrama most recently in Indonesia, India, England, Lithuania, Greece, Italy, Brazil and Italy. If you would like to attend one of her workshops to experience this process for either personal growth and training, please e mail, write or visit the website. She can be reached at www.souldrama.com or connie@souldrama.com. She would love to hear your comments about this book.

The International Institute of Souldrama
620 Shore Rd.
Spring Lake Heights, NJ 07762 USA

Made in United States
North Haven, CT
14 November 2022

26683577R00133